ECHOES

OF THE

COVENTRY

BLITZ

The Lady Godiva window, composed of pieces of stained glass from windows shattered in the Blitz, Holy Trinity Church. (Photo Gerry van Tonder)

ECHOES
OF THE
COVENTRY
BLITZ

GERRY VAN TONDER

PEN & SWORD HISTORY

To the unbroken spirit and the spirit of the unbroken.

First published in Great Britain in 2018 by
PEN & SWORD HISTORY
An imprint of
Pen & Sword Books Ltd
Yorkshire - Philadelphia

ISBN 978 1 52670 967 7

A CIP catalogue record for this book is available from the British Library

Typeset in 10/13 Sabon LT Std
Typeset by Aura Technology and Software Services, India
Printed and bound in India by Replika Press Pvt. Ltd.

Pen & Sword Books Ltd incorporates the Imprints of Pen & Sword Books Archaeology, Atlas, Aviation,
Battleground, Discovery, Family History, History, Maritime, Military, Naval, Politics, Railways, Select,
Transport, True Crime, Fiction, Frontline Books, Leo Cooper, Praetorian Press, Seaforth Publishing,
Wharncliffe and White Owl.

For a complete list of Pen & Sword titles please contact

PEN & SWORD BOOKS LTD
47 Church Street, Barnsley, South Yorkshire, S70 2AS, England
E-mail: enquiries@pen-and-sword.co.uk
Website: www.pen-and-sword.co.uk

Or
PEN AND SWORD BOOKS
1950 Lawrence Rd, Havertown, PA 19083, USA
E-mail: Uspen-and-sword@casematepublishers.com
Website: www.penandswordbooks.com

CONTENTS

The Rape of Coventry

Unbowed, undaunted, staunch, unconquered still,
The free men of the ancient town defy the Boche's will.

Not e'en the thirsty Dunkirk dunes,
Ed-slaked with British blood.
Which answer stern gave to the world
Of where this country stood.

Not e'en the heroes of the sea
Who gladly died to keep her free
Have scrawled their name on England's fame
Like thee, brave Coventry.

The mellowed stones which flanked the streets
When fair Godiva rode,
Now hallowed tombstones make for those
Whose death our life bestowed.

With aching hearts, but courage high
You faced a blitz of hate,
So ghoulish that no words would fit
Except 'To Coventrate'.

Yet points the city's noble spires
Unswerving to the skies.
From whence the desolation came
To where grim vengeance lies.

J.C.T.
The Midland Daily Telegraph, 15 April 1941

INTRODUCTION

'The bombing went on and on, for about 11 hours constantly. You'd occasionally hear the pom-pom-pom sound of the ack-ack [anti-aircraft guns] but the planes were so low overhead it was so noisy.'

Coventry Blitz survivor, September 2010

From August 1940, Hitler's Luftwaffe mercilessly and indiscriminately bombed cities and towns in Britain.

The historic West Midlands city of Coventry did not escape the carnage as, night after night, high-explosive and incendiary bombs rained down on the hapless production centre of cars, munitions and aero-engines. Then came Operation *Mondscheinsonate* (Moonlight Sonata), in which thirteen waves of more than 500 German Heinkel, Dornier and Junkers bombers sparked an inferno of hundreds of fires, including a devastating and uncontrollable firestorm.

On this fateful night of 14 November 1940, 4,400 homes were destroyed, while two-thirds of the buildings in the city centre sustained structural damage.

Today, the iconic shell of Coventry's once majestic medieval cathedral offers a silent memorial of remembrance to that dreadful night, for little remains of what was the inner city at the time of the Second World War.

For the city's residents of today, it is a poignant reflection of a violent and destructive part of their history. Almost eighty years on, few remain who might remember the Coventry Blitz.

Employing contemporary and modern images – mostly taken by the author – to compose contrasting compositions, and, drawing from contemporary press accounts and documents from the National Archives at Kew of the Coventry Blitz, this book presents a different, and to some extent unique comparative insight into the Nazi bombing of Coventry during the Second World War.

The real challenge for the author, however, quickly became apparent. While being shown around the city centre by local historians Rob Orland and David McGrory, it was very evident that almost nothing remains of the pre-war commercial districts with which to accommodate wartime images in a comparative manner. Very few landmarks have withstood the Luftwaffe, the revolutionary thinking of city architect Donald Gibson, and the ultra-modernism from the latter part of the twentieth century.

The young Gibson, who spent the fourth year of his studies and training at Harvard University in the United States, had, before the outbreak of hostilities, already decided that the city centre was hopelessly congested and overcrowded. For the far-sighted planner,

Modern Coventry map with an overlay of a War Office chart of the war, each dot representing a high-explosive bomb. Solid dots are for November 1940.

vehicular traffic and pedestrians were not able – and should not be allowed – to co-exist in the confines of a medieval market town centre. Gibson would be a pioneer in the concept of vehicle-free pedestrianized malls, or precincts as he referred to them. Ironically, and with great tragedy, Nazi dictator Adolf Hitler, and his promise to 'Coventrate' British cities, dramatically facilitated Gibson's vision for a new Coventry far quicker than he could ever have hoped for.

Coventry's trams would never operate again, so gone are the embedded lines. Streets have been re-aligned. In the immediate surrounds of Holy Trinity and St Michael's, for example along Bayley Lane, some of the historic has survived, but gone is the mid-nineteenth century St Michael's Baptist Church and the Free City Library a few paces away. The famous three spires held hope for providing perspectives, but such vistas are by and large now obscured by new buildings, especially multi-storey university edifices.

Erstwhile roadways – Hertford, Smithford, Market, Broadgate – are almost entirely impossible to identify, the pedestrianized precincts having profoundly altered the complexion of the inner city. And where an old landmark does still exist, matching the old with the new was problematic. A good example was looking along Bishop Street from its junction with Hales Street. On the corner stands the Old Grammar School, a magnificent stone building that has withstood centuries of change. At the end of Bishop, however, three tall concrete structures, the start of the city's latest property development, dwarf the street to such an extent, that they appear to truncate the thoroughfare.

When compared with other British cities targeted during the 1940–41 Blitz, Coventry is unique. Relative to its size, the city sustained the most structural damage. It was determined, however, that the restoration process would not emulate the historic. Radical new concepts of layout, architectural design and construction material would in every aspect metamorphose the city centre. Over time, some of the 1950s and 1960s structures also fell victim to the demolishers, as the Blitz-induced transformation continues unabated to this day.

For those who, like the author, find it difficult to imagine the horrific days of the Blitz against a modern tableau, it is hoped that the author's graphic journey will likewise transport the reader back to nights and days of fire, explosions, destruction, and the noise of enemy aircraft and that of the city's guns fighting back. Air-raid sirens and searchlights pierced the night, instilling unimaginable fear, then scouring debris and rubble to recover the living and the dead.

It is a window into a time and place that is difficult to picture.

TIMELINE

1939

2 September — Coventry Mayor Alderman S. Stringer declares that the city's police, fire brigade and Air Raid Precautions (ARP) have been placed on a war footing.

3 September — Britain declares war on Nazi Germany.

1940

5–6 June — Luftwaffe fighter aircraft commence probing sorties over Britain to test the strength of the RAF.

24 June — France yields to the invading German forces.

25 June — Coventry's first air-raid alert, but the Luftwaffe does not reach the city.

1 August — Hitler issues a directive: 'Overpower the English air force.'

12 August– 6 September — The Luftwaffe attacks fifty-three RAF airfields, predominantly in the south-east.

8 August — The King and Queen visit Coventry, inspecting industries and civil defence services.

19 August — *The Midland Daily Telegraph* reports that a German raider dropped a bomb in a city residential area the previous night. Due to censorship, the 'Midlands town' is not identified.

20 August — In the early morning, German bombers drop 'screamer' bombs on the city.

25–26 August — 'Raid Damage in Midland Towns: Cinema and Houses Wrecked', is carried on the *Telegraph*'s front page.

The RAF bombs north-west Germany, the Ruhr and Berlin.

Daimler's No. 1 factory is hit during a raid.

28 August — Coventry's first bombing fatalities occur in a raid over the Hillfields area. Buses are damaged and the Ordnance Works is hit.

4 September — Hitler promises revenge for the RAF bombing of German cities, heralding the start of the bombing phase of his attack on Britain.

15 September — Battle of Britain Day.

16 September — The Luftwaffe commences specific city bombings.

Houses in Coventry are damaged as German bombers try to target the Daimler Works.

In early October, the Luftwaffe switches to night-bombing raids to avoid RAF fighters.

12–13 October	The *Telegraph* headlines a 'Big Scale Raid on Midlands Town', during the night. Two Coventry policemen are reported killed in the raid. The first heavy raid takes place, causing considerable damage to the city centre.
14 October	A second heavy bombing raid.
19 October	A lone raider strafes installations and drops a few bombs.
19–20 October	A number of small raids hit several industrial targets, including Humber-Hillman, Armstrong Siddeley, GEC and Ordnance Works. Many civilian premises are also hit.
21 October	Referring to a raid the previous night, the *Telegraph* headlines 'Intense Raids on Midlands Town: Houses Demolished and People Entombed'.
22 October	Holy Trinity Church and St Mary's Guildhall are hit.
25 October	The newspaper headlines 'A sharp attack of short duration on one Midland town', during the night, i.e., Coventry.
26 October	Aero-engine factories on Parkside and properties in Aylesford sustain bomb damage.
29–30 October	St Lawrence's Church and vicarage and domestic properties are damaged in the Foleshill area.
1 November	A lone raider bombs the Silver Street area, causing fatalities and considerable damage to buildings.
3 November	Whitley, Foleshill and the London Road Pumping Station are bombed.
7 November	German bombers again raid Foleshill.
12 November	Further raids in the Foleshill area. The Directorate of Home Operations receives intelligence of the Luftwaffe's Operation Moonlight Sonata, but believes this to be against London and the south-east.
14–15 November	The devastating 'Moonlight Sonata' bombing raid on Coventry.
16 November	The King and Queen visit Coventry.
19 November	A brief raid over the Earlsdon and Cheylesmore areas of Coventry.
20 November	The first mass burial of 172 people killed in the bombing.
23 November	In a second mass burial, 250 are interred.

1941

8–9 April	German bombers conduct a 'double attack' during the night.
10–11 April	Widespread damage as Coventry endures a relatively short attack.
15 April	A further 394 victims of bombing raids are interred in a mass grave in the London Road Cemetery.
26 September	Premier Winston Churchill visits Coventry.

1942

25 February	The King and Queen visit Coventry.
30 July	A stray bomber kills three on Bulls Head Lane – the city's last bombing fatalities.
31 August	The Luftwaffe conducts its final raid over Coventry.

1
WHY COVENTRY?

'The German air assault on Britain is a tale of divided counsels, conflicting purposes, and never fully accomplished plans.'

Winston Churchill, *The Second World War* (Reprint Society, 1951)

Although adjacent to the doomed St Michael's Cathedral, Holy Trinity Church survived the war, in no small measure thanks to the dedicated and extremely dangerous vigil of the church clergy and their fire guard on top of the lead-covered roof.

In the foreground is the Coventry Cross, a replica of the original 1544 Tudor cross (pictured below). Unveiled in 1976, the structure stands on the corner of the site where the John Gulson Free Library was before being badly damaged during the Blitz.

The unimaginable! Deadly Luftwaffe Heinkel He 111 bombers over Coventry. (Photos Bundesarchiv and Gerry van Tonder)

In July 1940, Hitler's commander of the Luftwaffe, Reichsmarschall Hermann Göring, assumed direct and personal responsibility for the air war over Britain. His Führer demanded the annihilation of the Royal Air Force as an imperative prerequisite to Operation Sea Lion, his planned invasion of the British Isles. For fifty-seven consecutive nights, the aerial onslaught on London was relentless, as successive waves of German bombers launched their terror from nearby bases in France and Belgium.

In just six weeks from 10 May 1940, the blitzkrieg tactics of Hitler's *Wehrmacht* and Luftwaffe steamrolled across Western Europe towards Britain, subjugating the Netherlands, Luxembourg, Belgium and France as they went. This provided a massive strategic advantage for Hitler who, while peering through binoculars at the English coast, instructed Göring, to bring the isolated island nation to its knees with his Luftwaffe.

Hitler's Directive No. 16 required the hamstringing of Britain's aerial defences to pave the way for an invasion in mid-August – Operation Sea Lion. The German dictator's Operation *Aldertag* – Eagle Day – was implemented to destroy the RAF.

The Battle of Britain, from July to October 1940, contested mainly over the south-east, dispelled the myth of the Luftwaffe's air superiority. Hitler's bid to bring Britain to the negotiating table by bombing the island nation into submission had failed. Unable to neutralize Fighter Command, Göring diverted his attentions to the RAF on the ground: air stations and ground installations. At the same time, the Luftwaffe started to target Britain's war industries, bombing the factories that fed the nation's war machine. By September, the tactic of terror-bombing followed, in what Göring referred to as 'strategic bombing'.

Luftwaffe aircrew prepare for a raid across the English Channel, a Dornier Do 17 in the background, armed and fuelled for the mission. (Photo Bundesarchiv)

With the logistics of long-distant bombing sorties yet to be mastered, the RAF, in a very limited way, struck back at Berlin. In the last week of August, the RAF 'attacked important military objectives in the city', described by the Air Ministry News Service as 'including aircraft factories, aerodromes and lighting instillations'. Hitler was furious.

'If they attack our cities,' he threatened on 4 September, 'we will simply erase theirs.'

The unsustainable losses of September saw the Luftwaffe switching its operations to night raids, and by the following month, the Blitz had become a nocturnal phenomenon. London was no longer the only major target as other ports and industrial centres drew the attention of the German night bombing raids. Liverpool was targeted on the Atlantic, while Hull's geographical position made the city a ready dumping ground for bombs from aircraft that had failed to locate their objectives in the night. Bristol, Cardiff, Portsmouth, Plymouth, Southampton and Swansea followed as targets, as well as the industrial heartland cities of Birmingham, Belfast, Coventry, Glasgow, Manchester and Sheffield.

Germany lacked adequate intelligence on Britain's war industries, which meant that the bombing raids were never constituted as a clear strategy by the Luftwaffe High Command, the *Oberkommando der Luftwaffe*. After eight months of bombing, British war production remained strong.

Operations *Loge* (codename for London) and *Seeschlange* (sea snake) heralded the bombing offensives against London and other industrial cities. On the nights of 14 and 15 October, *Luftflotte* 3 (air fleet) conducted the heaviest night raids on London to date. According to the Luftwaffe, during the month more than 8,000 tons of ordnance had been dropped on the capital – 90 per cent at night – while Birmingham and Coventry were subjected to 450 tons in the last ten days of October.

In spite of the absence of a clear-cut formal strategy, the Luftwaffe adopted a predominantly nocturnal 'routine' of sustained attacks on London, while continuing to execute night raids on the West Midlands' war materiel factories. In addition, fighter-bombers would perform random daylight raids on the same targets. *Luftflotte* 3 was ordered to fly 100 nightly sorties over the West Midlands.

Civilian casualties in the months of September and October alone were in the tens of thousands, giving substance to the contention by a growing number of international observers that the German bombing was indiscriminate, failing to hit military targets.

On the night of 3 November, the air-raid sirens remained quiet in a tense but unyielding London. The following night, the Luftwaffe turned its attention to the British industrial heartland. While London would remain a prime target, and with his planned invasion mothballed, Hitler sought to bomb Britain's industrial cities, thereby crippling the essential war effort.

Strict black-out regulations were applied to buildings, vehicles, cyclists and pedestrians alike. A consequence was a significant increase in the number of injuries and deaths linked directly to the stringent rules. Compounded by the requirement that streetlights remain switched off, pedestrians being struck by cars constituted the greatest number of black-out casualties. Drivers of motor vehicles, including those of the emergency services, their vehicle headlamps almost totally obscured and pointing downwards, found it extremely difficult to spot pedestrians out at night. For the discerning motorist driving a Coventry-made upmarket car, specially manufactured black-out hoods could be clamped on to their car's headlamps (pictured opposite).

(Photo Gerry van Tonder)

According to local media, the black-out phenomenon was turned to the advantage of the city's industries:

FACTORIES DARKENED FOR ONE HOUR ONLY
Coventry's big 'black-out,' after all doubts and difficulties, is to turn out happily for all concerned.

Factories will obtain practically 100 per cent of their normal night-shift production, while the workpeople will lose nothing in wages.

Now, the factories will be completely darkened for the first hour, until 1 a.m. During this time the various night shifts will take their meals and then carry on normally after 1 o'clock.

The decision at yesterday's meeting concerns 50 organisations employing approximately 60,000 people.

It will be during this first hour that the greater part of the exercises of the defence organisations will be carried through. Representative groups of all the services in the city will be on duty doing practical training under conditions as near approaching those of war as peace-time can produce.

'Casualties' caused by the 'bombs' of raiding aircraft have been arranged and these will bring into action the emergency medical service.

For the exercise on Thursday only No. 1 first-aid post at the Gulson Road Clinic will be manned. A fleet of ambulances will be ready at the post and when notification of the 'casualties' is received the first-aid parties, with ambulances and nurses, will drive out with dimmed lights to bring the 'injured' back for treatment.

The Midland Daily Telegraph, Tuesday, 11 July 1939

A year earlier, Hitler had entered into a non-aggression pact with Stalin, purely as a ruse by the German dictator so that, with no distractions to the east, he could concentrate on achieving his principal goal of subjugating the whole of Western Europe, including Great Britain. The much-despised Bolsheviks would only then receive his full attention, and the Soviet races obliterated from the planet as part of his master plan to secure *lebensraum* for his Aryan tribe.

For the last two months of 1940, the Blitz ceased to be the exclusive domain of the British capital, as, among others, the cities of Coventry, Birmingham, Liverpool, Sheffield, Manchester, Leeds, Leicester and Glasgow fell prey to German bombs.

War premier Winston Churchill, in his seminal work on the Second World War, comments on Coventry's fate:

These new bombing tactics began with the blitz on Coventry on the night of November 14. London seemed too large and vague a target for decisive results, but Goering hoped that provincial cities or munition centres might be effectively obliterated.

The raid started early in the dark hours of the 14th, and by dawn nearly five hundred German bombers had dropped six hundred tons of high explosives and incendiaries. On the whole this was the most devastating raid which we sustained. The centre of Coventry was shattered, and its life for a spell completely disrupted. Four hundred people were killed and many more seriously injured.

The German radio proclaimed that our other cities would be similarly 'Coventrated'.

Nevertheless, the all-important aero-engine and machine-tool factories were not brought to a standstill; nor was the population, hitherto untried in the ordeal of bombing, put out of action.

For many, the ancient city of Coventry is perhaps more synonymous with the legendary Countess of Mercia, Godiva, riding naked through the medieval streets of this West Midland town, as a mark of protest against unfair taxation.

For a long time the nation's premier ribbon-maker, from the late nineteenth century Coventry gained considerable prominence as a hub of motor car and cycle production, industries which spawned ancillary manufacturing of machine tools, mechanical chains and engine parts. Daimler, Standard, Triumph, Humber, Hillman, Singer, Sunbeam, Rover and Massey Ferguson became household names.

Established in 1896, The Daimler Motor Company Limited went on to produce this quaint 1898 yellow and black car (pictured opposite), characterized by wooden, spoked wheels and solid rubber tyres Following financial difficulties, Birmingham Small Arms Company (BSA) acquired Daimler in 1910.

Founded in 1903, the Standard Motor Company established its first assembly factory in Much Park Street. In 1907, Charles Friswell became chairman of Standard, immediately enhancing the profile and status of the company. In 1907, the Standard Roi de Belges car came off the line. This one on display in the Coventry Transport Museum (pictured opposite),

Above: 1898 Daimler.
(Photo Gerry van Tonder)

Right: 1907 Standard.
(Photo Gerry van Tonder)

is believed to be the first one produced, hence the SMC 1 number plate. Targeted at the Edwardian wealthy, the wooden body was handmade and trimmed with brass and leather. The Roi de Belges was powered by a 2l six-cylinder engine, giving the car a comfortable cruising speed of 40mph. Standard provided seventy cars for King George V and his entourage at the Delhi Royal Durbah in 1911. The following year, Standard was acquired by C. J. Band and Siegfried Bettmann, founder of the Triumph Motor Cycle Company, that later became the Triumph Motor Company.

Singer Motors Limited, founded by George Singer in 1874, started bicycle production in Coventry under the name Singer and Co. From 1901, Singer added motor cycle and three-wheeled vehicle production to its growing business. The first four-wheeled car rolled out in 1905.

Daimler took great pride in its prestigious vehicles, such as this 1935 Daimler 50, Queen Mary's personal royal limousine, and her personal property from new until 1953. The engine is an impressive 6.5l V12 cylinder. George V was driven about in a 1929 Double Six 30 Daimler, while Winston Churchill used a 1932 Daimler Barker, complete with a bulldog bonnet mascot.

With the outbreak of hostilities in Europe in 1939, an insatiable war machine demanded that British industry diversify into the essential production of aircraft, vehicles, equipment and

A Singer. (Photo Gerry van Tonder)

Queen Mary's Daimler 50. (Photo Gerry van Tonder)

munitions to stem the continental spread of Nazism. For industrial Coventry, the needs of the Air Ministry became a priority.

First established in 1909 as Siddeley Autocars, successive acquisitions and mergers resulted in the emergence in 1919 of Armstrong Siddeley Motors Ltd, manufacturers of luxury motor cars. By 1935, engineering interests were further incorporated with Avro, Vickers and Hawker, strengthening Armstrong Siddeley's core business of aero-engine production.

The company would also produce army staff cars, ambulances and trucks. The sprawling works, including Burlington, was situated within a half-mile radius of the city centre, south and adjacent to what is today the Ringway, St Johns.

The Armstrong Siddeley seven-cylinder radial aero-engine, the Cheetah X, was first introduced in 1935, with production only ceasing in 1948. The highly successful air-cooled engine powered RAF trainers during the war, including the Avro Anson and the Oxford Airspeed.

The Standard Motor Company Ltd works stood at Hearsall Common, Canley, less than two miles west of the city centre. Founded initially to produce marine and motor engines, in the First World War the Canley site, opened in July 1916, produced more than 1,000 Royal Aircraft Factory B.E.12s and R.E.8s, Bristol F.2 two-seat biplane fighters, and Sopwith Pup biplane fighters. The heavy-engineering facility also turned its hand to the production of shells and trench mortars. During the Second World War, Standard manufactured its most famous wartime product, the de Havilland Mosquito aircraft, mainly the FB VI variant, of

The Cheetah X. (Photo Ian Dunster)

which more than 1,100 were turned out. The company's status as one of Coventry's top war effort contributors was attained through the added production of 750 Airspeed Oxfords, 20,000 Bristol Mercury VIII aero-engines and 3,000 Bristol Beaufighter fuselages.

Extolling the right to strike back at Nazi headquarters' buildings in Berlin, the de Havilland Mosquito is depicted (following page) as the instrument of retaliation while appealing to the British population to financially endorse the nation's war machine. Almost entirely constructed of wood, the Mosquito was a front-line multi-role combat aircraft. Also used for high-altitude reconnaissance, as well as forming the backbone of the Light Night Strike Force used as pathfinders in Bomber Command's heavy-bomb raids over Germany, the aircraft first went into production in 1941. It also performed a key defensive night-fighter role and was employed as air support for the British army's Normandy landings in 1944. It was only in the 1950s that the RAF retired the omnipotent aircraft.

In the 1920s, the Alvis Car and Engineering Company commenced motor-car production from Holyhead Road in Coventry, specializing in four- and six-cylinder engines. Having shortened its name to simply Alvis Ltd in 1936, at the outbreak of the war the company added

R.A.F. day raiders over Berlin's official quarter.

BACK THEM UP!

(Ministry of Information)

Rolls Royce Merlin engine. (Photo Gerry van Tonder)

the manufacture of aero-engine and armoured-vehicle divisions to its portfolio. Importantly, during the war, Rolls-Royce in Derby sub-contracted Alvis to produce superchargers for a dozen of its Merlin aero-engine marks. Fitted to Spitfire and Hurricane fighters to provide maximum power at altitude, Rolls-Royce regarded the supercharger as key to the success of the Battle of Britain.

While continuing with car production in the Second World War, the company entered into the production of the de Havilland DH.98 Mosquito and Airspeed AS10 Oxford, mainly used for training Commonwealth aircrews, including in the colonies. Also produced were Bristol Mercury VIII radial aero engines, Bristol Type 156 Beaufighter multi-role aircraft, and the Beaverette standard light armoured car, the latter seen here sporting the ubiquitous Bren machine gun.

In the late 1920s, the Rootes brothers, William and Reginald, diverted their highly successful distribution and servicing entrepreneurial skills to the motor manufacturing industry, acquiring well-known brands such as Hillman, Humber, Sunbeam, Talbot and Commer.

Under the Air Ministry's 'shadow' factory plan, in 1940 Rootes Ltd constructed an enormous aero-engine production and assembly plant at Ryton-on-Dunsmore, some five miles south-east of Coventry on what is now the A45.

The enduring pride of the Rootes group turned out to be the 1943 Humber used by Field Marshal Bernard Montgomery as his staff car from the Allied D-Day landings on 6 June 1944 to the end of the war in Germany. Standing in the front of his Humber, the war supremo leads a convoy of his troops across the Seine at Vernon on 1 September 1944 (pictured opposite). Berlin was still a very long and very costly way ahead. Logging more than 60,000 miles in twelve months, the appropriately christened *Victory* – Montgomery referred to it as 'Old Faithful' – was transported back to Britain in July 1947. The formation emblem on the car's left fender is that of the 21st Army Group, of which he was commander. The 4.5l, six-cylinder

Right: Beaverette standard light armoured cars. (Photo Max Smith)

Below: Montgomery, standing in his Humber, leads his troops across the Seine. (Photo Sgt Morris)

(Photo Gerry van Tonder)

Humber is now on display in the Coventry Transport Museum (pictured above), courtesy of the Peugeot Motor Company.

The government scheme allowed for the in-house transfer of motor-production skills to aircraft production. The Humber/Hillman Motor works was situated in an area bound by Humber Road, Sunbeam Way and Aldermoor Lane to the west, south and east respectively. After acquiring the site in 2012, Network Rail erected a national distribution centre. In a straight line, the cathedral is only a mile from where the works once stood.

Just to the east of the Humber/Hillman works was the GEC Telephone Works. As wartime production demand increased, including that for two-way radios for fighter planes and radar for night-fighters, additional factories were acquired in Spon Street and Queen Victoria Road. Today, the Odeon and Ikea occupy these sites.

Originally established in 1903 to produce naval ordnance, the Coventry Ordnance Works (COW) was recommissioned in 1936 for the manufacture of gun mountings. Hemmed in by the canal to the south and Red Lane – off Stoney Stanton Road – to the north, during the First World War COW had developed and manufactured the 4.5in. howitzer, the COW biplane and the 5.5in. naval gun.

Production of the 15in. siege howitzer at the 60-acre site during the Great War was prolific, women playing an important production role in the barrel shop. The post-war recession had a profound negative effect on the works, resulting in Coventry selling its Glasgow works in 1920 to Harland and Wolff, the famous builders of the *Titanic*. In 1925, the works was forced

THE COVENTRY ORDNANCE WORKS LIMITED

H.M.S. AJAX.

ARMAMENTS

Works:

COVENTRY   SCOTSTOUN   CLIFFE

(near Glasgow).

Range: BOSTON (Lincs.)

London Office:
3, CENTRAL BUILDINGS, WESTMINSTER, S.W.

(Photo morgana)

Naval guns in production at the Coventry Ordnance Works. (Photo Rob Orland)

Coventry Ordnance Works gun workshop. (Photos Horace Nicholls and Gerry van Tonder)

to close down. The government's national rearmament programme in 1936 saw the works recommissioned to manufacture gun mountings, for which it already had the machine tools to rejig for the new production.

Just to the north of COW on Helen Street, was Rover Motors, Coventry works. Founded by Messrs Starley and Sutton in 1878, the first Rover was a humble bicycle. Eastern Europe proved to be a lucrative market, where the legacy of the company's bicycle

The 1920 Rover motorcycle. (Photo Yesterdays Antique Motorcycles)

The 1914 Rover 123 Tourer. (Photo Peter Turvey)

may be found in the Polish *rower* and the Belorussian *rovar*. At the turn of the century, Rover experimented with producing a motor cycle, scrutinizing Peugeot motorcycles for inspiration. Come the First World War, the company had confidently created their own motorcycle, selling their 499cc model to the Russian army. The development of a range of cars more or less paralleled that of Rover's motorcycles. Emulating almost all the large engineering companies in Coventry, Rover took up pre-war gas-turbine production. Sustaining considerable damage during the Blitz of 1940 and 1941, the Helen Street works would never again reach full production, selecting instead to concentrate its resources in 'shadow' factories at Birmingham and Solihull.

Although Rover set up shadow factories for the production of aero-engines and airframes in Birmingham and Solihull, the main works in Coventry sustained major bomb damage in 1940 and 1941, resulting in the facility never regaining pre-war levels of production. Rover also had a factory near those of GEC on Queen Victoria Road. In a straight line of flight, the GEC and Rover factories were a scant 400 yards from the cathedral.

At the start of the war, the Triumph Motor Company, facing financial ruin, was purchased by a third party, but fate determined that the company would not rise again. The company remained in production up to this point, such as this 1934 Triumph light-delivery van (pictured below). Motor car production was suspended, and in 1940, the works on Holbrook Lane was totally destroyed by the Luftwaffe. The Standard Motor Company would purchase the 'Triumph' brand name at the end of the war.

A 1934 Triumph 8cwt light van. (Photo Charles01)

Above: The Modern Machine
Tools factory in the 1920s.
(Photo www.lathes.co.uk)

Right: (Photo www.lathes.co.uk)

Founded in 1921, the eponymous Modern Machine Tools Ltd had two production sites in Coventry. One, within a half-mile radius of the city centre, was situated just above where the Central Six Retail Park stands today. The other was farther west, in the Chapel Fields area. Manufacturing a range of state-of-the-art machine tools, including capstan lathes, boring machines, gear-shaper attachments, tube-forming mills and siphon pumps, the company became integral to Coventry's war production.

The Coventry Chain Company was situated in what is now the Arches Industrial Estate, Spon End. The company was first established in 1896 in Dale Street as a manufacturer of bicycle chains. The Meteor Works in Coventry was among the city's bicycle manufacturers to pioneer rear-wheel chain-driven bicycles. Developing and producing track chains during the First World War, the company simultaneously promoted its revolutionary 'noiseless' chain. A merger with Hans Renold Ltd in 1930 saw the company's name changed to reflect the amalgamation: Renold and Coventry Chain Co. Specializing in the revolutionary multiple-application bush roller chain – still in use today in vehicle and aircraft engines, and on motorcycles and bicycles.

Daimler was by far the giant of Coventry's war production. Owned by the British conglomerate, the Birmingham Small Arms Company Limited (BSA), during the Second World War, produced more than 9,000 of the diminutive 2.5l 'Dingo' scout cars and 4.1l Daimler armoured cars for the British army. The larger Daimler sported a 2pdr quick-firing gun. Tank components were also manufactured, including 2,500 epicyclic gearboxes.

(Photo Starley)

Daimler 'Dingo' scout car. (Photo Copyleft)

Daimler armoured car. (Photo Gerry van Tonder)

Bren light machine gun. (Photo Sergeant Laing)

In keeping with a mainstream activity of its parent company, during the war Daimler produced 74,000 .303 Bren light machine guns. The main support weapon of British and Commonwealth forces during the Second World War, the Bren was also very effective mounted on armoured vehicles or in an anti-aircraft role when mounted on a tripod. With its diagnostic forward-curving magazine, the Bren was one of the most reliable weapons of the war, and was still being used in the Falklands War in 1982. When the weapons' workshop was destroyed in the April 1941 air raid, production shifted to Burton upon Trent.

Much of Daimler's wartime production was dedicated to the manufacture of aircraft components. The production included almost 51,000 Mercury, Pegasus and Hercules model Bristol radial aero-engines, propeller shafts for Rolls-Royce aero-engines, and more than 14,000 bomber gun-turrets, complete with .303 Browning machine guns. The Mk II variant was the standard machine gun fitted to RAF aircraft during the Second World War. Wing-mounted on Supermarine Spitfires and Hawkers Hurricanes – heroes of the Battle of Britain – the Browning was also either hand-operated or turret-fitted in bombers.

Daimler operated two works' sites. The original Sandy Lane works, Bishopgate Green, was gutted during an incendiary-bombing raid on the city. The works was only half a mile from the cathedral. The other was just to the north in the area where the sports amenities are on Alverley Road.

Singer Motors Limited, the name adopted by the new owners in December 1936, had a long history of manufacturing in Coventry, from bicycles in the 1870s, to motorcycles and engines, and four-wheel motor cars from 1905. By the late 1920s, Singer had grown to

Armourers install .303 Browning machine guns into the rear turret of an Armstrong Whitley. (Photo B. J. Daventry)

become Britain's third largest producer of cars after Austin and Morris. As with others in the car-manufacturing industry in Coventry, and indeed throughout the nation, Singer converted its assembly lines to war production.

Sub-contracted to manufacture weapons' components, such as .303 rifle sights and bolts, the company ran two factories: one just above the A4600 on Hood Street, and the other nearby on Vine Street, to the east of the National Express depot. The sites were less than half a mile from the cathedral. For Singer, the war years were far less lucrative compared with the halcyon days of motor-car production for the general public. Bombed during the war, sadly, for Singer those days would never return.

To the north of the city centre, on Foleshill Road, stood J. J. Cash Ltd (Cash's) weaving factory, which was damaged during bombing raids on the city. The company still exists in Coventry.

Farther out on Foleshill Road, was Courtaulds. Established in 1794, the company became the world's leading manufacturer of artificial fibres.

Albeit labelled strategic, the very nature of bombing is indiscriminate, even in the modern era of accurate guided devices. 'Unintentional' collateral damage to civilian property and life is inevitable. The 1940–41 scenario in which the city of Coventry found itself was profoundly compounded by the extremely close proximity to the city centre of numerous war-production entities, significantly increasing the vulnerability of non-war-related infrastructure and citizenry.

There can, however, be no doubt that Adolf Hitler cared little – if at all – about where his bombs fell, prompting a Coventry resident, in November 1940, to refer to 'Hitler's devilish resolve to raze the city to the ground'.

Left: Lee Enfield .303 infantry rifle. (Photo Sergeant Lambert)

Below: J. J. Cash Ltd premises before the war. (Photo morgana)

Manufacture de J. & J. Cash, Ltd., à Coventry.

The pre-war Courtaulds factory. (Photo morgana)

On the front page of the Friday, 15 November 1940 edition of the *The Midland Daily Telegraph* – the future *Coventry Evening Telegraph* – there appeared a report on a German radio broadcast:

COVENTRY PAYS FOR MUNICH

Nazi radio:

Apart from London, and other targets of military importance [the announcer stated], Coventry – the centre of the British aircraft industry – was raided by waves of strong forces of German bombers.

Early in the evening [14 November 1940] bombs of the heaviest calibres were dropped on numerous aircraft engine works and aircraft accessories' plants.

At 9 p.m., more than 20 large fires lit the way for the following bombing squadrons, which continued their attacks throughout the night.

The defences were helpless against the vigorous attack of the Luftwaffe.

The increasing fires caused big explosions, indicating that not only factories but also large stocks of raw materials, some manufactured goods, and finishing products had been destroyed.

In the final analysis, Coventry was unquestionably a major contributor to Britain's national war production. This fact was no secret to Nazi Germany, so the hapless city was like a magnet to Hitler's forces of destruction. The greatest tragedy was, of course, that Coventry's war industry was physically situated within a civilian conurbation. Trams, motor cars, bicycles, people – the epitome of a vibrant and alive Coventry of the 1930s.

Broadgate south view, 1930s. (Photo Rob Orland)

With the outbreak of hostilities, however, was the unsuspecting Coventry prepared for enemy attack from the air?

MORE PUBLIC AIR RAID SHELTERS

Public shelters at present completely ready in the centre of Coventry number two, and will accommodate a total of 770 persons. Five more nearing completion will probably be approved within the next 24 hours. They will accommodate approximately a further 730 people, bring the total number of persons for whom satisfactory provision can be made up to 1,500.

These figures provide striking support for the urgent appeal to the citizens to shop near home made by the City's National Emergency Committee. The appeal was made because, whereas thousands of people, particularly at the week-ends, are still flocking into the central shopping area, public shelter in the city centre can be provided only for a few hundred people.

Close to the central shopping area, but not near enough to be of use in providing cover for people who may actually be in the vicinity of Broadgate when an air raid warning is given, are three other completed public shelters accommodating together 962 persons. These are trenches at Primrose Hill Park (250 persons), Bird Street (312 persons), and a basement shelter at the Corporation's Leicester Road Depot (400 persons).

The Midland Daily Telegraph, Wednesday, 13 September 1939)

2
TOOLS OF DESTRUCTION

It must be borne in mind that, so far, this has been a war of pursuit planes, fighters, and reconnaissance machines. Relatively few bombing squadrons were used even in Poland. Hitler's main bombing fleet remains locked in its underground hangars somewhere in Germany.

When will it be used? No one can say. Is Hitler holding his punches, waiting for the psychological moment to hurl the full force of his vast armada at Allied capitals? That, too, remains to be seen. But there is no reason to suppose that heavy Junker bombers and the Heinkel machines are any better than the Messerschmitt fighters which our pilots have already driven on to the defensive. Nor that the R.A.F. will fail to at least equal the Nazi bombers' performances.

There are said to be 19 separate defences to London and our other big cities. Our defence system has a nasty surprise for any enemy armada which crosses the British coastline.

Robert Wishart, *Aberdeen People's Journal*, Saturday, 7 October 1939

The mainstay of the Luftwaffe's bomber fleet were the Heinkel He 111, Dornier Do 17 and Junkers Ju 88, employed for bombing at medium to high altitudes. The Junkers Ju 87 Stuka was recognized for its terrifying dive-bombing tactics. However, the slow and therefore vulnerable Stuka suffered significant losses during the Battle of Britain, so was largely withheld from the British Blitz campaign.

Operating from bases in France and the Netherlands, Göring's *Luftflotte* 2 and 3 bombers deployed over Coventry comprised the Dornier Do 17Z, Heinkel He 111 and Junkers Ju 88 light and medium bombers. Each aircraft had varying capabilities: the He 111 was the slowest of the three, while the Ju 88, once it had disposed of its payload, was the fastest. The Dornier had the lightest bomb load. All required fighter escort protection, usually in the form of the ubiquitous Bf 109 Messerschmitt.

Targeting the West Country, the Midlands and north-west England, Luftwaffe battle wings, or *kampfgeschwader*, comprising two to three squadrons, or *gruppen*, were based at individual airfields. For example, *Kampfgeschwader* 54, made up of two squadrons of Ju 88s, was based at Évreux, in Haute-Normandie in northern France, 260 miles from Coventry.

Between 1939 and 1940, 1,700 variants of the Dornier Do 17Z twin-engine light 'Flying Pencil' bomber were produced. Armed with up to seven 7.92mm MG 15 machine guns, the four-crew bomber had a bomb payload of 2,200lb. Having made its battle debut during the Spanish Civil War in 1937, the limited capabilities of the Do 17 accounted for its demise as a front-line bomber by the end of 1941.

Luftwaffe over Coventry

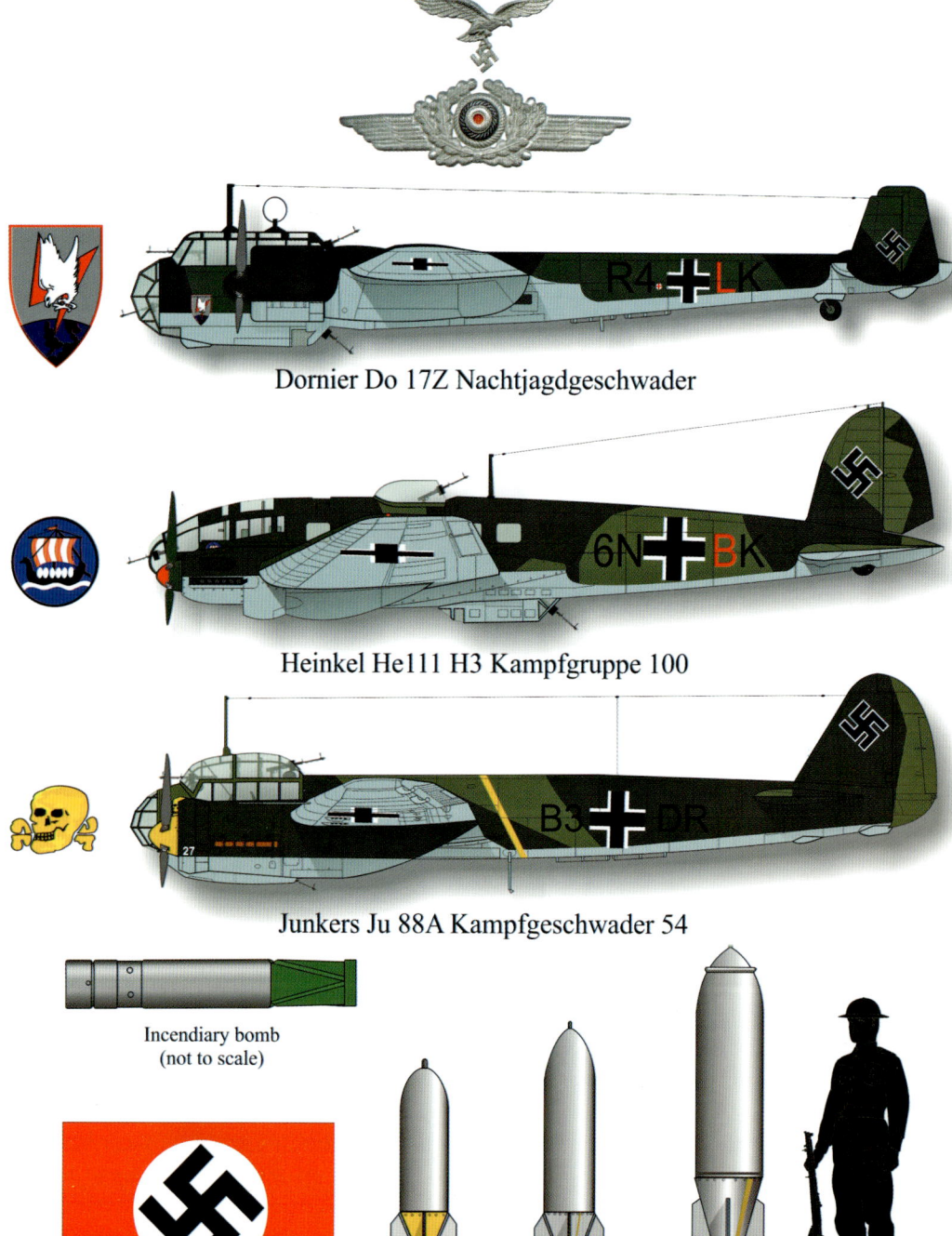

Dornier Do 17Z Nachtjagdgeschwader

Heinkel He111 H3 Kampfgruppe 100

Junkers Ju 88A Kampfgeschwader 54

Incendiary bomb
(not to scale)

SC 50   SC 250   SC 2000

(Courtesy Colonel Dudley Wall)

Dornier Do 17Z. (Photo Bundesarchiv)

Heinkel He 111H. (Photo Bundesarchiv)

Junkers Ju 88. (Photo Bundesarchiv)

Developed in 1934 under the guise of a civilian transport, the Heinkel He 111 was the Luftwaffe's most prolific bomber during the early stages of the war. Used in far greater numbers than the other bombers reconnaissance variants of the He 111 accompanied them on their missions. With an internal bombload of 2,200lb, the medium bomber's armament included a 20mm MG FF cannon, a 13mm MG 131 machine gun and three 7.92mm MG 81Z machine guns. Of the 1,260 built in 1939, a crippling 756 of these aircraft were lost during the Battle of Britain. More than 5,600 Do 17s were made until September 1944, when production ceased.

The Junkers Ju 88, which first flew in December 1936, was regarded as the most versatile German military aircraft of the Second World War. Dubbed a 'fast bomber', or *schnellbomber*, over 16,000 Ju 88s and variants were built. The Ju 88's multi role capabilities included that of dive-bomber, fighter-bomber, heavy fighter and night-fighter. The four-crew aircraft had a bombload of 4,400lb. The plane could be armed with a combination of up to six 7.92mm MG81 and 13mm MG131 machine guns.

After France capitulated, Germany regrouped its *Luftflotte* – air fleets – facing southern and northern England. Initially, *Luftflotte* 2, under Generalfeldmarschall Albert Kesselring, was responsible for raids on south-east England and London. *Luftflotte* 3, commanded by Generalfeldmarschall Hugo Sperrle, targeted the West Country, Wales, the Midlands and north-west England. *Luftflotte* 5, under Generaloberst Hans-Jürgen Stumpff targeted the north of England and Scotland from his base in Norway. As the bombing progressed, target responsibilities changed, with *Luftflotte* 3 assuming greater responsibility for the night-time raids, while the main daylight operations rested with *Luftflotte* 2.

The efficacy of the RAF to defend British skies was, in the early part of the war, an issue of much debate:

GERMAN BOMBERS ARE 'COLD MEAT'

'The mistake some of our pilots made at first,' said a flight-leader, 'was in loosing off with our guns while the German bomber was still a couple of hundred yards away. If you wait until he is within 50 yards – when he looks like an enormous bat in your sights – the first burst will cut him to ribbons.

'The result is usually dramatic and often instantaneous. I've seen them crumple up within a second.'

While German bombers having been playing havoc in Norway, just because our fighters have been unable to get at them it is the right time to take a tonic from the men who count – the 'chaps' who sit behind the Hurricanes and Spitfires and gossip about the much-vaunted Dorniers as though they were pigeons.

I can assure you that the attitude of the average fighter pilot to-day is that of the sportsman with a 12-bore gun who goes out at dusk after homing birds. His problem is how to get within range and not how to avoid counter fire – how to keep the bomber from escaping into the clouds and to position himself with 50 yards of his tail.

'I've hunted around the clouds chasing bashful Germans on many occasions,' said another [pilot], and when he spoke I could not help thinking of a fox terrier after a rat in a chicken run. The metaphor has changed from pigeons to rats – but both analogies hold good.

Newcastle Journal, Friday, 10 May 1940

The bombs these aircraft dropped over Coventry and its environs were mainly high explosive (HE) and incendiary, together with a range of specialized devices. Commonly, composite payloads of HE and incendiary were carried, on the premise that the explosive bombs would ignite stored materials of a flammable nature.

'Cigar' for Churchill from Göring. (Photo Bundesarchiv)

The *sprengbombe cylindrich*, designated SC, thin-cased, general-purpose bomb was generally the chosen ordnance in the early stages of the war. Almost 80 per cent of the bombs dropped over Britain were of this type. These were mostly of the SC50 (50kg) and SC250 (250kg), fitted with both short- and long-delay fuses. Larger bombs were also used when there was a need, such as the SC1000 (1,000kg) 'Herman' or the SC1800 (1,800kg) 'Satan'.

Typically, SC bombs were either filled with a 60:40 Amatol/TNT blend, or a variable mixture of TNT with wax, woodmeal, aluminium powder, naphthalene and ammonium nitrate additives.

Another class of bomb was the medium-cased *sprengbombe dickwandig*, designated SD, which came in 50, 70, 250, 500 and 1,700kg sizes. These were semi-armour-piercing and mainly used on 'hard' targets such as shipping, naval installations and coastal fortifications.

For night raids, which was generally the case over Britain, 50kg parachute flare devices, LC50s, were dropped for target illumination and marking.

Designed to cause maximum blast damage in built-up areas, the Germans also employed adapted sea mines, referred to as landmines by the Civil Defence. Fitted with descent-retarding parachutes, the mines came in two sizes: the 5ft-8in.-long 500kg *luftmine* A, and the 8ft-8in.-long 1,000kg *luftmine* B. Detonating above the ground, the mines caused considerable damage to buildings.

Within the Luftwaffe's aerial arsenal were two types of incendiary devices: magnesium and oil bombs. In the blitz over Britain, it was largely the former, a 1kg bomblet known as a *brandbomb*, the 1kg *electron*, with the designation B1El. It was made up of a magnesium alloy (elektron) cylinder with an incendiary filling of thermite. Ignited on impact by a percussion charge in the nose, the resultant heat was great enough to melt steel.

German 1kg incendiary bomb.
(Photo Gerry van Tonder)

Early in the war, expendable containers, each with a capacity of thirty-six B1Els, were used to dispense the bomblets. These *abwurf behalter* or *bombenschaltkasten* containers conformed with the dimensions of a standard SC50 bomb, which meant that a Heinkel He 111 could be armed with four of these containers, amounting to 1,152 incendiary devices. Bombloads, however, were usually mixed. As the war progressed, re-usable containers were developed, ultimately with a capacity of 620 bomblets.

Used more extensively on Coventry was the phosphorus incendiary bomb or *phosphorbrandbomb*, a device with the same dimensions as the SC50 and SC250 HE bombs, but filled with phosphorus, oil and rubber solution. On impact, phosphorus carried in a glass bottle would break and mix with the rest of the filling. As the bomb casing split, the spontaneously ignited contents would spray over a large area.

The *flammenbomb*, referred to simply as the oil bomb, a blend of oil and explosive charges, was the original large incendiary device. Based on the 250 and 500kg bomb cases, and designated *Flam* 250 and *Flam* 500, they proved unreliable as the impact fuses often failed to detonate on impact. As a consequence, their general use was withdrawn at the beginning of 1941.

During the worst bombing raid on the night of 14/15 November 1940, Luftwaffe bombers dropped 500 tons of HE, 50 air-mines, 20 oil-mines and a staggering 36,000 incendiary devices over Coventry.

Britain was totally unprepared for the defence of the nation at night. Searchlights were underpowered and ineffective above 12,000ft. In July 1940, the whole country had only

Junkers Ju 88. (Photo Bundesarchiv)

Ordnance QF 3.7in. anti-aircraft gun. (Photo Gerry van Tonder)

550 light and 1,200 heavy anti-aircraft guns deployed at defensive sites. Of the heavy-calibre weapons, 200 were of the obsolete 3in. type. At this early stage of the war, limited technology meant that there were very few night-fighters to take on the German bombers.

Coventry's air defences that night comprised twenty-four Ordnance QF 3.7in. (94mm) anti-aircraft and twelve 40mm (1.575in.) Bofors guns. The 'quick-firing' 3.7in. fired a 28.56lb shell with an effective ceiling of 32,000ft.

The Swedish-made Bofors was one of the most successful weapons of its type ever produced, earning itself virtual legendary status. Firing a 1.96lb shell, with a ceiling of 23,600ft, the gun had a cyclic rate of fire of 120 rounds per minute.

The city's anti-aircraft weaponry expended a massive 6,700 rounds – some emplacements ran out of ammunition – but only managed to down one German bomber.

Barrage balloons during the war were regarded as a major deterrent to low-flying German aircraft, particularly bombers. Filled with lighter-than-air gas, the balloons were set at desired, often staggered, heights, tethered by cables onto ground winches or static fixtures. A Balloon Command was formed in Britain in 1938, comprising 52 barrage balloons squadrons, and by August 1940, more than 2,300 operational barrage balloons were in strategic positions over vulnerable cities and towns. Ultimately, Balloon Command reached a strength of 33,000 throughout the UK.

Apart from one German bomber clipping a balloon cable with its wing, there is no tangible evidence to suggest that Coventry's barrage balloons did anything else but present German pilots with a bit of an annoyance.

(Photo B.J. Daventry)

Bofors 40mm anti-aircraft gun. (Photo Gerry van Tonder)

Barrage balloons over Coventry's High Street. (Photo Gerry van Tonder)

3
PRELUDE: JUNE–SEPTEMBER 1940

'It screamed downward, splitting air and sky without effort. A target expanded in size, brought into focus by time and velocity. There was a moment before impact that was the last instant of things as they were. Then the visible world exploded.'

Steven Galloway, *The Cellist of Sarajevo*

19 JUNE 1940

German bombing raids over Britain during the night of 19 June were reported as being the biggest to date. More than 100 bombers, it appeared, compared to the previous night, that the Luftwaffe was now after industrial targets in the north-west and South Wales. Across the country, sirens sounded: from the south coast, around the eastern seaboard, and all the way up to Scotland. Six civilians died and sixty were injured, but damage to industry was light. Five days later, reports came in of raids in the Midlands in which three elderly people were injured when their cottage in the small village of Pailton near Coventry was hit. Buried in the rubble of their home, neighbours managed to extricate the three shocked occupants. The local school sustained damage when two bombs exploded in front of the building. In a house opposite, an RAF officer and his wife escaped injury when a large chunk of shrapnel flew through their bedroom.

8 AUGUST 1940

On 8 August, the Royal train arrived in Coventry, bringing the King (George VI) and Queen for a visit to the Alfred Herbert and Coventry Gauge and Tool works. Dressed in the khaki

Junkers Ju 88 dropping its payload over Broadgate. (Photos Bundesarchiv and Gerry van Tonder)

uniform of a field marshal, at the King's first factory stop a guard of honour was provided by the works' Home Guard. Employing over 6,500, a third of whom were women, the staff showed their appreciation of the Royal support by repeatedly drumming their benches, adding to the din of hundreds of machines. At the second factory, the King proved he was worthy of his uniform by scoring a 'bull' at the works' rifle range for Home Guard training.

18 August 1940

About an hour before midnight on Sunday, 18 August 1940, the stillness of a sleeping Coventry was shattered by the baleful wail of air-raid sirens. A lone, winged harbinger of Hitler's Luftwaffe roared over Canley and Cannon Hill, dropping fourteen high-explosive bombs.

Twelve houses in a partly developed housing estate on the outskirts of the city sustained blast damage, but miraculously, and considering the time of night, not even minor injuries were reported. Most of the bombs detonated in neighbourhood gardens and surrounding fields, while two landed on roads.

One couple later spoke of how they had been suddenly woken by an ear-shattering explosion followed by a violent shaking of the house. As the man tentatively opened their bedroom door, the moon shone on his face – the bedroom opposite was no longer there. The house received an almost direct hit, completely demolishing half the house. The only damage to the room in which they had been blissfully asleep only moments before, was a crack in one of the walls.

School children sift through rubble against a backdrop of post-war housing. (Photos Rob Orland and Wikimedia)

A short distance away, a semi-detached house sustained far greater damage. Fortuitously, there was no one home. With her husband, an army officer based in another town, away, the woman and their 3-year-old daughter were spending the night with her mother in a nearby town. The little girl's cot was found half buried under rubble, while her playpen was found in the huge crater made by the bomb at the side of the house. In the neighbour's house, their baby daughter remained asleep, their house escaping any major damage.

A short distance down the same road, the roofs and windows of two houses were damaged when two bombs fell in the back gardens. In one house, large pieces of bomb debris shot through the bedroom window and over the bed in which a couple had been sleeping. Afterwards, the 67-year-old wife commented stoically, 'When you get to my age, you take what is coming to you and are glad it was not worse.' Different people reacted differently to the experiences of having endured – and survived – Hitler's bombs, resulting in the relating of such events becoming a popular topic of conversation.

20 AUGUST 1940

In the early hours of Tuesday, 20 August, nine bombs fell over Coventry, including, for the first time, the terror-instilling 'screamer' bombs. During the war, the Luftwaffe routinely attached various devices to bombs that would make them 'scream' or 'whistle' as they fell. With the sole purpose of enhancing the terror being experienced by those on the ground during a raid, cardboard organ-type pipes or flute-like metal bomb tail whistles affixed to bombs provided the desired terrifying scream.

The towers of the Coventry University Library overlook the remains of an Anderson shelter. (Photos Ministry of Information and Rock drum)

Speaking afterwards to a reporter from the *The Midland Daily Telegraph*, an old army veteran, who at the time was in an Anderson shelter with three other adults and five children, related how he had said, 'Quick – cover your ears and set your teeth.' Even then, they could not block out the petrifying scream that grew progressively louder. They believed that they were going to take a direct hit. Amazingly, however, all they heard was a 'soft thud which seemed to be half a mile away'. It had in fact fallen only 50yd from where they had sought refuge. That night, most of the bombs detonated harmlessly across a field.

At the outset of the Blitz, it had become abundantly clear that incendiary devices were integral to the Luftwaffe's bombing strategies of the British Isles. Civil awareness of the nature of the bombs and how to deal with them became a priority for the dissemination of information from several government ministries and agencies:

PUTTING PAID TO FIRE BOMBS
When you are fighting fire-bombs, which ones should you tackle first?

The answer in most cases is the fire-bombs that fall indoors. These are the bombs which, left alone, are almost certain to start big fires; whereas dozens of the incendiaries that fall in the open will burn themselves out without doing much harm.

So when fire-bombs are falling in your district, don't rush out at once to deal with them in the open. Remember a fire-bomb may have penetrated your own roof without you hearing it. Make a careful search of top floors of any building for which you are responsible, and don't go out till you are certain that all is well indoors. The possible danger from a fire-bomb in the open is a small matter, compared with the blaze that will result if an unsuspected fire-bomb is left to set a whole house alight.

Suppose you find a room on fire, get busy at once with the stirrup pump. Don't be put off if the room seems an inferno – it is surprising how much smoke and heat you can get from a small fire. A stirrup pump used properly is many times more powerful than it looks – you will be astonished to find how big a fire-fighting job it can tackle.

Coventry Standard, Saturday, 7 June 1941

Notwithstanding sustained efforts by the city's air defences, large high-explosive bombs and incendiary bomblets caused major damage to suburban houses, three schools and manufacturing premises. Casualties were numerous, including the death of two people when a street shelter took a direct hit, and a further two when a building collapsed.

While emergency services addressed immediate critical needs, volunteer groups of rescuers visited demolished buildings to search for survivors. One such team spent six hours digging and tunnelling into the rubble of a three-storey building that had sustained a direct hit. In the narrow confines of crude hand-dug passageways, the rescuers discovered a badly injured woman. The tunnel was cleared to allow a doctor in to administer morphine to facilitate easier extraction. Once she was out, the arduous and dangerous brick-by-brick tunnelling recommenced.

The next victim was a young boy, trapped by his legs. The space was so restricted, and with any further clearing at this spot deemed too hazardous, the doctor had to instruct the volunteer who had found the boy how to administer morphine to the hapless youngster. The team would go on to find a third person alive.

Searching for life. (Photos Ministry of Information and Wikimedia)

An impossible task. (Photos Ministry of Information and Gerry van Tonder)

At another such rescue scene, a 14-year-old girl tirelessly, and without fear, ensured that a rescue team opposite her home did not go without mugs of hot tea. It was reported that, even when a big bomb exploded nearby, she did not spill a drop!

This was the third night raid in succession, but this did not deter the fire brigade and volunteers from tackling fires and attending to the injured, even while the raid was in progress. By first light, the main fires had been extinguished and the endless cleaning-up process started afresh.

On the 22nd, German radio confirmed that Birmingham, Coventry and Liverpool had been bombed in 'retaliatory' raids. The communique added that 'fires and explosions were observed in plants of military importance'. The *Telegraph* also reported on a daylight raid by two German aircraft on two Midlands towns, in which the bombers flew 'low enough for their markings to be plainly seen'. In the first town, five bombs fell in the gardens between two rows of houses, damaging seven properties. A volunteer of the AFS spoke of seeing one of the aircraft dive-bombing a factory and being met with machine-gun fire from the ground. The bomber then unsuccessfully strafed the ground with his machine guns.

24–25 AUGUST 1940

A 'sharp attack' on the night of the 24th saw the scattering of incendiary bombs preceding a drop of high-explosive bombs in which several houses, two air-raid shelters and a pub were damaged. There was damage to gas and water mains and a disruption of electricity supply to some areas of the city.

The magnanimity and community-mindedness of Coventry's citizens took the immediate edge off the pain and suffering endured by so many. In the darkened confusion of hosepipes, noise, rubble and dust, townsfolk could be seen handing out comforting hot drinks to anyone in need, while selflessly offering accommodation to those who had just lost their homes.

There was no thought given to the danger of falling masonry or from delayed-action bombs. A *Telegraph* reporter heard from 85-year-old Mr Abrahams how, when an incendiary bomb had dropped into his kitchen, and using only a handkerchief for protection, he had picked up the bomb and placed it in a bucket of water. In spite of burned hands, he had then taken care of the fire caused by the device.

In its Monday, 26 August 1940 edition, the *The Midland Daily Telegraph* reported on 'waves' of bombers that had conducted raids in the Midlands during the night that were the 'most widespread and intensive ... since the war started'. Adhering to strict censorship, the daily newspaper only mentioned 'a Midlands town' in its reference to Coventry.

The city's Rex Cinema sustained severe damage, but luckily the theatre was unoccupied at the time. A bomb penetrated the roof and detonated in the auditorium, collapsing almost the entire roof. The main part of the cinema was reduced to a shell, with only the large girders remaining in one piece. From the debris-littered projection room, very few of the auditorium seats could be seen. Had the bomb blast occurred an hour later, the casualties would have been great. In a lucky twist of fate, the night watchman had been given the night off. Ironically, the popular Hollywood hit *Gone with the Wind* was due to have had a debut screening that very Monday.

Not a great distance from the wrecked cinema, an enormous delayed-action bomb exploded, flinging slabs of road surface into the air. The debris smashed through the roofs of two shops opposite, completely demolishing the buildings. Nearby, occupants of a bomb

Modern Coventry University buildings rose from acres of bombed-out properties. (Photos Rob Orland and Snowmanradio)

An anti-aircraft gun lights up a gloomy Coventry. (Photos Lieutenant Tanner and Gerry van Tonder)

shelter related afterwards how the rippling vibrations from the explosion threw them about in the shelter. Bricks and other debris could be heard falling on the shelter's roof. The 15ft-deep and 30ft-wide crater was rapidly filling with water from a fractured main.

Shops and houses were damaged, while fifty incendiary devices fell in a suburb. As the AFS attended to the resultant fires, they were machine-gunned from the air.

Over several hours, five waves of German bombers pounded Coventry, while searchlights and anti-aircraft batteries desperately tried to defend the city from the seemingly endless aerial onslaught.

In addition to widespread damage to domestic properties, the Baddeley & Co. factory in Lower Ford Street was gutted by fire and Kenning & Son in West Orchard badly damaged. The Market Hall was also razed to the ground, and with no hope of saving the building, all firemen could do was to contain the blaze to prevent it from spreading to the fish market and nearby shops. Incredibly, there were no fatalities, and only eight people required hospital treatment for injuries received during the raids.

In the city centre a delayed-action bomb was discovered in the proximity of an old cottage. Police hastily evacuated residents in the immediate area to safe shelter, with the exception of one obstinate man who refused to leave his home and had to be manhandled to safety. A while later, the bomb detonated, leaving a large crater. There were no casualties.

A badly damaged machine shop at the Armstrong Siddeley Works. (Photo courtesy © Rolls Royce Heritage Trust, Derby)

Elsewhere, incendiaries rained down in an area on the city's outskirts. Most fell into open ground, while property fires were quickly brought under control by the AFS and civilians alike using stirrup pumps.

An incendiary had started a substantial blaze in a building contractor's yard, acting as a beacon for a following wave of bombers. As firemen fought the fire, fresh bombs started to fall. The men found shelter, however, and there were no casualties.

The German radio boasted that the Luftwaffe had bombed 'aircraft factories and armament works'.

25–26 AUGUST 1940

The following night, a 'number of high-explosive bombs and hundreds of incendiaries' fell from the German raiders. The largest fire broke out at a timber yard, while others ignited at a warehouse and a grocery provisions merchant. A suburban school was also set ablaze, serving as a marker for the night bombers. In a now typically indiscriminate pattern, bombs fell on a golf course, sports fields, near a home for orphans, and close to several factories.

Following up that morning on an unconfirmed report that a Dornier bomber had been brought down by anti-aircraft fire and three parachutes spotted, searches in a cordoned-off area found no trace of any such incident.

In a sobering first for the battered city, casualty lists from the weekend attacks were posted in public on a sidewall of Council House on Earl Street (pictured below).

(Photos David McGrory and Gerry van Tonder)

An anti-aircraft searchlight team, with the Coventry cathedral's spire in the background. (Photos Lieutenant Taylor and Gerry van Tonder)

28–29 AUGUST 1940

On the night of 28 August, Coventry endured a lengthy period of expansive bombing. As parachute flares descended, bombs started to fall in a 'working class' area of the city, resulting in fatalities. Several homes suffered structural damage and a gas mains was ruptured. In one house, seven residents had a miraculous escape while cowering under the stairs. A bomb struck the roof, causing it to collapse inwards. Only one person suffered any injury, and that was slight.

It would only be twelve hours after an elderly couple was reported as missing that rescuers found their bodies under the stairs, the house relatively undamaged – the couple had succumbed to a gas leak. Elsewhere, the residents of one wrecked house had been sheltering in their newly acquired Anderson shelter which had only been erected that Sunday. Though the shelter was hidden by debris, they were dug out without injury.

There was now a growing concern among the authorities that people were being unnecessarily injured when standing in the open, gazing at the spectacular pyrotechnics being provided by German parachute flares, searchlights and the paths of anti-aircraft fire. On this particular night, some people were killed while they stood on a road watching the raid.

30–31 AUGUST 1940

On 30 August, several Midlands towns over a wide area experienced their first raids of the Blitz. An interesting development in the German ordnance was also noticed for the first time. In order to cut back on the more expensive magnesium in their incendiary devices, the Luftwaffe had started to use petrol instead.

For Coventry, the next fortnight was a period of relative respite, while London and the south-east received most of Göring's attention.

SEPTEMBER 1940

In early September, the RAF raided Berlin with fire-bombs on four consecutive nights, stating that military targets in the Reich capital were being targeted. The latest raid had been unexpected as there was thick cloud cover and it had been raining. Bombs fell near the Brandenburg Gate at the western end of Unter den Linden, while others fell in the Tiergarten. The German media reported civilian deaths. During this period, there was an easing of the intensity of bombing over the Midlands. This, however, did not slow down the wheels of the Nazi propaganda machine. On Tuesday, 3 September, the *The Midland Daily Telegraph* reported on a German High Command communiqué issued the previous day:

COVENTRY MUNITION WORKS BOMBED
On September 2, our bombers and fighters attacked enemy aerodromes in the South of England. Hangars and aerodrome buildings were damaged by direct hits from bombs in Hornchurch, Gravesend, Eastchurch, and Detling.

A number of fights developed, in which our 'planes were victorious.

Night attacks by our 'planes were directed against English West and South Coast ports, munition works in the Midlands, and aerodromes. Bombs were dropped in the ports of Liverpool, Swansea, Bristol, Plymouth, Portland, Poole, and Portsmouth, and on munition works in Birmingham, Coventry, and Filton. Large fires were started at many points.

8–9 SEPTEMBER 1940

Meanwhile, the RAF increased its own aerial pressure on Nazi Germany, conducting a three-hour raid on Hamburg on the night of the 8th. From 10 p.m., RAF bombers launched wave upon wave of sorties over Hamburg, dropping heavy-calibre, high-explosive bombs and hundreds of incendiaries. Homing in on the River Elbe, the Blohm & Voss yards were turned into seas of fire. Wharves and railway stations on the river's northern reaches suffered the same fate. From sixty miles off, as the bombers headed for home, they could see the glare over Hamburg. Three nights later, it was the turn of Berlin.

16–17 SEPTEMBER 1940

On the night of Monday, 16 September, three waves of German bombers flew over Coventry. Reporting on the events of that night, the *Telegraph* spoke of eight bombs having been dropped, destroying six houses 'in a purely residential district far removed from anything resembling a military objective'. There were children among the fatalities suffered that night on Stevenson and Wallace roads, north of the city and some three-quarters of a mile from one of the Daimler works. It was believed at the time that one of the bombs was an 'aerial torpedo', which had deflected off a road before ploughing into a block of houses.

The demand for bomb shelters escalated dramatically:

12,000 ANDERSON SHELTERS IN COVENTRY
Large numbers of people are still making application in Coventry for Anderson shelters, but, although recently the authorities were informed that a further 2,000 were on their way, there is no purpose in any fresh requests being made.

The new supply is already exhausted, preference having been given to those who made applications for Andersons before the Government stopped the supply of steel, and to special cases where there is serious illness.

There are now about 12,000 domestic Anderson shelters in Coventry, and work is proceeding as rapidly as labour and material considerations will permit on the erection of street-side domestic surface shelters. About 27,000 applications have been made for brick shelters.

The Midland Daily Telegraph, Monday, 2 September 1940

For many of the city's residents, however, it was the sight of a low-flying, twin-engine German Junkers Ju 88 bomber that would be remembered most. According to eyewitnesses, the bomber had clipped a barrage-balloon cable, followed shortly thereafter by exploding and crashing into a field between the villages of Walsgrave and Withybrook to the east of Coventry in 'a ball of fire'. Upon realizing that they were going down, the pilot had jettisoned his load of eight heavy-calibre bombs – the ones responsible for the carnage on Stevenson and Wallace roads.

According to an eye witness, at the top of Stephenson Road a bomb – believed to be a torpedo bomb – demolished a row of four houses (58–64), killing all but two of the residents.

Six houses down, the blast caved in the door of a family's Anderson shelter, at the same time piling rubble on top of the roof. Upon being rescued, and calmed by a few cigarettes, the home owner spoke of being met outside by a scene from hell. Houses, sheds and fences had disappeared, and on the road a burst gas main was burning furiously. For him though, the most poignant sight was seeing dust-covered bodies being carried away on stretchers. One was of a woman two houses down, her arms still around her equally lifeless baby.

Anderson Shelter in a Coventry suburb. (Photos Ministry of Information and Snowmanradio)

(Photos Wikimedia and Gerry van Tonder)

In a bizarre incident not far away, a bomb exploded next to two wooden garages. One was reduced to firewood, the car inside crumpled, while the garage next door received only slight damage and the car inside did not even get a single scratch.

An off-duty AFS man said later that he had seen the German aircraft make a 'pot-hook' turn when hitting the balloon cable followed by what he thought was the sound of machine-gun fire. He only just managed to run back inside his house when an enormous explosion shook the whole house. The door, blown in by the blast, fell on top of him. As he stumbled, he knocked his wife over and fell on top of the cooker. A second explosion followed, which he reckoned lifted the cooker three inches off the ground. After the raid, he ventured back outside to find the two houses opposite his completely destroyed.

Home Guard (the new Coventry Cathedral provides a backdrop to the Coventry Home Guard pictured above) and military personnel immediately attended the crash site, where they were unable to rescue two German crewmembers from the burning wreckage. The other two crewmembers had managed to parachute out in time and were apprehended. One had sustained a broken leg and the other an injured ankle.

A debate ensued over the cause of the Ju 88's demise, with some claiming that it was as a result of anti-aircraft fire, while others said they had seen an RAF fighter on the tail of the bomber.

For the city, maintaining good spirit and morale was imperative in the midst of the frightening loss of loss and property, and the uncertainty of what might happen tomorrow or the next day. Distractions were a therapeutic necessity:

NEW HIPPODROME
Don't try to analyse the new show 'Flying High' at the New Hippodrome, Coventry, this week. (Some people are excessively fond of sorting over a show and picking at it like epicures.) Just sit back and enjoy it.

A gas-masked ARP warden below the Cathedral spire. (Photos Ministry of Information and Gerry van Tonder)

There is an abundance of entertainment material for every type of patron. In the humour section there is the infectious grin and boisterous tomfoolery of Maurice Colleano, who would turn a somersault at you as soon as wink. In his fun production he has able assistance from his brothers and sisters, Rubye, Joyce, Bonar, George, and Lindsay.

If you like dancing, keep an eye open for Gold and Cordell – of who we see too little.

Archie gets us into the spirit of the show in quick time, and Elsie Bower sways the crowd with her singing and piano-playing.

Another item to enjoy is the guitar number of Al Bowlly and Jimmy Mesenes.

Although Coventry's air-raid sirens sounded periodically and ARP wardens patrolled the streets as German bombers flew overhead, no more bombs fell on the city for the remainder of that September. The trials of the proper Blitz, however, were only weeks away.

In London, speaking in the Commons, Prime Minister Churchill warned that a German invasion was imminent.

4
MOONLIGHT SONATA

'We have had to do with the long range, heavy German bomber alone. Taking day and night together, nearly 400 of these machines have, on the average, visited our shores every 24 hours. We are doubtful whether this rate of sustained attack can be greatly exceeded. No doubt concentrated effort could be made for a short time, but this would not sensibly affect the monthly average.'

Winston Churchill, 7 October 1940

Wartime premier Winston Churchill. (Photo British Government)

As the winter nights started drawing in, there was a lull in Luftwaffe activity over Coventry. There had been several air-raid alerts, but these tended to be spontaneous preparations as unseen German bombers rumbled overhead on their way to strategic targets in either the north-west or in other centres in the Midlands.

12–13 OCTOBER 1940

In the Saturday, 12 October edition of *The Midland Daily Telegraph*, it was reported that Coventry City FC was sitting comfortably at sixth out of the thirty-four clubs in the South Region league, and the local GEC rugby team had managed to arrange home and away games. Godiva Harriers were finding that the Sunday morning runs were growing in popularity, reminding readers that there would be another run that Sunday, the 13th, starting at 10 a.m. at Butts Ground. Also on the Sunday, three semi-finals of the Parcels Fund Lawn Tennis Tournament would be played at Binley Road, near the GEC Works.

That very Saturday night, with a bright hunter's moon lighting up the sky, the Luftwaffe returned. At a Luftwaffe airfield in France, in 1940 a concrete sign had been imbedded in the runway, the destination of the night raiders based there ominously clear (pictured below).

Described by the *Telegraph* as a 'big scale enemy air attack on a Midlands town', successive waves of German bombers dropped hundreds of bombs and around 300 incendiaries, of both the magnesium and oil type, over Coventry in a raid that lasted two hours. Most of the bombs fell on residential properties and in fields. Among those killed were two policemen, two wardens and a member of the AFS, all while performing their duties during the raid.

Police Constable William Henry Leadham, aged 36, and Sergeant James Arthur Fox, 37, had been evacuating around 200 people from the Crane's Hotel at the top of Bishop Street where a delayed-action bomb had been discovered, when a pub where they were standing took a direct hit from a high-explosive bomb. Both policemen were killed instantly.

Air Raid Precaution wardens Phillips and Williams were killed when a bomb exploded in Stamford Avenue. Former serviceman and AFS messenger H. F. Willoughby died in hospital after a bomb exploded next to his station, burying him under large chunks of clay.

(Photo Rock drum)

(Photo Rob Orland and Snowmanradio)

Most of the large industrial works had their own fire brigades. A bomb-damaged Armstrong Siddeley property stands behind the fire engine. (Photos courtesy © Rolls Royce Heritage Trust, Derby and Gerry van Tonder)

As Sunday dawned, tales of bravery, dedication and sheer luck started to circulate.

For their bravery and dedication to duty Campbell Joseph Kelly OBE, MC, MM, Control Officer, Works Air Defence Department, and David Lloyd, First Officer, Works Auxiliary Fire Service, were awarded the George Cross and the Medal of the Civil Division of the Most Excellent Order of the British Empire, for meritorious service, respectfully. Their citation reads:

> Mr Kelly's organisation and personal bearing have been largely responsible for the building up of a highly efficient Works Air Raid Defence team.
>
> His personal activities on the night of an intensive air raid were largely instrumental in saving his factory from destruction. He extinguished an incendiary bomb and immediately afterwards took twelve volunteers to help the City Fire Service deal with a serious fire. After that, they attended at another fire and on the way back helped to extricate the bodies of policemen who were trapped in debris left by high explosive bombs.
>
> A large high explosive bomb hit a works shop but fire was avoided by prompt action under Kelly's guidance.
>
> Until five o'clock in the morning Kelly continued to give inspiring leadership to his men. There was no cover for any of the working parties and they all carried out what was asked of them with fortitude and courage.
>
> Mr Kelly was ably assisted in this work by David Lloyd, First Officer of the Works Auxiliary Fire Service.
>
> *The London Gazette*, 24 January 1941

Regular services members, volunteers and civilians alike threw themselves into the ongoing mayhem. Atop a pile of rubble that was once a block of houses, a shirtless man with no head protection laboured for hours through the masonry and broken timber, rescuing live women and children. He chose to ignore the bombs dropping around him. When praised, the man stoically responded by saying that he 'did nothing more than anyone else would do.'

AFS volunteer Wright had a narrow escape when a piece of shrapnel penetrated his steel 'battle bowler', as helmets were commonly referred to, and exited between his forehead and the helmet rim. While sustaining a bad scalp wound, Wright lived to tell the tale.

At a neighbourhood fire station, two members of the force were caught on the top of the station tower when a high-explosive bomb struck about half way up the structure. Escaping injury, one of the firemen, disoriented in the choking dust and smoke of the explosion, and believing he was on the ground, stepped out into open space. He fell 20 feet, smashing bones in both feet. His colleague made his way down without any mishap.

Two air-raid shelters took direct hits during the raid. One shelter, built to hold sixty people was, oddly enough, unoccupied at the time. In the second blast on a street shelter, fatalities resulted in both the structure and surrounding houses.

Members of the city's police force were arguably more vulnerable than most as they had to remain on duty in the streets. When a bomb exploded close to a police car, the occupants stumbled out their vehicle, but were only 'shaken'.

In another part of the city police officers were injured when sections of a damaged building fell on them. Elsewhere, three policemen eluded death when two bombs detonated close to

The AFS worked tirelessly in extreme conditions. (Photo Ministry of Information)

(Her Majesty's Stationery Office)

Destruction of the city centre was extensive. (Photos Lieutenant Taylor and Gerry van Tonder)

them in quick succession. A sergeant found himself flung through the air but, undaunted, he continued with his duties.

In the city centre, incendiary devices fell on the roof of Council House, while an adjacent shopping arcade's glass roof took a direct hit, spraying lethal shards of glass in all directions. In an incident laced with irony, an incendiary bomb fell next to a Luftwaffe Messerschmitt fighter, which formed the centrepiece of a display that was part of the national drive to raise war funds. The City Arcade took a direct hit from a high-explosive bomb, causing major damage to retailers, Messrs Adams. The shop fronts in the arcade were all blown in. A bomb detonated in the fire station drill yard, resulting in significant damage to the fire tower. Bombs fell on Warwick Road, Queen's Road and along Bishop Street. Twenty-two Corporation buses were damaged. The New Hippodrome narrowly missed destruction when Matterson's next door took a direct hit.

Elsewhere in the city, two bombs exploded in the cathedral churchyard, but only causing superficial damage. The Coventry Motor Mart on London Road and the Swift skating rink were razed to the ground in out-of-control blazes. The Rex Cinema, already badly damaged from a previous raid, took a direct hit, while on Foleshill Road, Hogarth Shoes took several high-explosive bomb hits. The majority of the buildings at the Stoney Stanton Road Tungsten Carbide works were destroyed.

One of the most remarkable stories from that night was of the courage and physical endurance of Irishman Michael Conway. A Coventry resident of ten years, Conway was huddled together with another fifteen to twenty others when their tightly packed shelter took a direct hit from a high-explosive bomb.

A typical concrete-roofed street shelter. (Photo Ministry of Information)

The brick-walled, concrete-roofed structure was completely levelled, trapping the occupants under a large pile of smouldering rubble. Drawing on every ounce of his physical strength, Conway tunnelled his way to the outside, where he immediately set about the seemingly impossible task of searching for other survivors. His wife, who had suffered a head wound, was the first one he dragged out, followed by his 12-year-old daughter.

His hands raw and bleeding, the exhausted Conway's efforts were unrelenting. Continuing unaided, Conway extricated his 6-year-old daughter next, and as he lugged masonry off the pile of debris, he freed another two children and two men – alive.

Responding to a call at the far end of the shelter, Conway found that he was unable to move heavy sections of walling that blocked his way. Finally, he staggered off to look for help, returning a while later with four soldiers. With bombs still raining down over the city, the five men used ropes to haul away slabs of masonry as best they could. When they could do no more, Conway started digging into the soil and rubble with his bare hands to reach a woman and her baby. He eventually succeeded in removing the injured mother and child from where they had been entombed.

Then, accepting that there was no more he could do, Conway carried his injured wife away to seek medical assistance. Thirty-one people died that night. The fire services received more than 200 call-outs.

Pedestrians walking in the direction of the council house clock tower (upper right) survey the night's destruction. (Photos Rob Orland and Gerry van Tonder)

14–15 OCTOBER 1940

On the following Monday night, 14 October, the German bombers returned over Coventry. Still coming to terms with the destruction and death only two days before, the city cowered as 'hundreds of bombs' fell during several waves of bombers, totally destroying forty houses and killing fifty-three people. In one incident, it was apparent that a torpedo bomb had destroyed or severely damaged a row of low-income houses. At the Coventry and Warwickshire Hospital, while stretcher bearers and medical staff attended to the flood of bombing casualties, incendiary bombs fell around the building and in the courtyard. Mercifully, the hospital was not hit.

In a residential street, a high-explosive bomb detonated between two Anderson shelters, which at the time held a total of eight people. In spite of the shelters collapsing to a width of only 2ft 6in., seven walked out without a scratch. The eighth person succumbed. At another collapsed house, a man had been sleeping on the ground floor when a bomb fell next to the property. In yet another amazing escape, the man found himself in the only space in the pile of rubble in which someone could have survived. It was with great difficulty and determination that he managed to claw his way out from where he was entombed. In another suburb, seven occupants of an Anderson shelter, including four children, were dug out from underneath a pile of debris in which they had become trapped inside their shelter on the edge of a cavernous bomb crater.

During the raid, civilians readily volunteered to assist with dousing incendiary devices. One young boy, perhaps foolishly so, managed to extinguish two incendiaries before a warden dragged him into a street shelter. Labourers at a lodging house left the relative safety of their building to attend to 'showers' of incendiary bombs that were falling in their street. Using their hats or any container they could find, and even with their hands, the gang managed to put out every fire, thus preventing any damage to the area. So pleased were they with their successes that they offered to assist elsewhere.

In another part of the city, a like-minded woman did not have the same measure of success. Standing by her bedroom window, she saw an incendiary bomb burst on the roof of an adjoining shop that was unoccupied at the time. With great presence of mind she fetched her stirrup pump and endeavoured to tackle the incendiary from the window. Sadly, her efforts were in vain. The incendiary burned through the roof, creating a blaze that gutted the building.

On Broadgate, the hub of the city centre, the relatively new Owen Owen departmental store building took a direct hit from a large high-explosive bomb. Penetrating through three levels, the bomb exploded, causing massive damage. Fortunately, the store was vacant at the time and the basement shelter withstood the blast. A nearby open-air market was also damaged.

On Greyfriars Lane, the iconic city landmark, Ford's Hospital, received a direct hit. Dating back to the start of the sixteenth century, the teak-and-oak-framed Tudor almshouse, remarkably, remained standing (pictured opposite). Tragically, the explosion claimed eight lives: the warden, a nurse and six elderly female residents. Six others were injured.

Nearby St Michael's, Coventry Cathedral, had an incendiary bomb penetrate the thick lead roof to start a fire on the wooden structure two feet below. Situated where it was, between the two roofs, fire services struggled to reach the spreading blaze. Wary of the ongoing conflagration around them, firemen clambered to the top of the building where they broke windows through which they stuck their hoses. Pews and carpets suffered water damage, but, for now, this magnificent medieval place of worship would survive.

At first light, reports were received that the city's opera house was ablaze. It was believed that the fire was either caused by a smouldering incendiary or by a delayed-action bomb.

(Photos David McGrory and Gerry van Tonder)

(Photos Rob Orland and Gerry van Tonder)

The three-year-old stage was gutted, while the auditorium sustained smoke damage. The fire station was hit again, and the Rex Cinema bombed for a third time.

School caretaker William Henry Patstone was awarded the George Medal for his unselfish endeavours at his place of employ. His citation read:

> During a severe enemy air attack the basement of a Girls' School was used as a shelter by members of the public. Patstone took charge of the shelter and those using it. H.E. bombs were falling in the district and there were many fires. The school was struck by a bomb and a fire broke out. Patstone climbed into the rafters and fought the fire for some considerable time despite the fact that bombs were dropping nearby. Many houses were demolished and Patstone took the homeless into the school shelter, inspiring them by his coolness and courage, particularly when the entrance was damaged. On two occasions, he was blown down the steps into the shelter by blast. This did not deter him from attending to the protection of those persons present and of the property.
>
> *The London Gazette*, 4 March 1941

The latest raid, in which it was clear that heavier calibre bombs had been employed, added a further fifty-three names to the growing list of Coventry citizens killed in the Luftwaffe raids.

Unexploded German bomb. (Photos Gerry van Tonder)

18 October 1940

Delayed-action and unexploded bombs posed the greatest danger, especially to those whose sole job was to attend to such unstable ordnance. The discovery of an unexploded bomb near West Orchard Chapel in Chapel Street on Friday, 18 October, would have very tragic consequences.

Second Lieutenant Campbell, Royal Engineers, drove over from Quinton Road base with his team from the 9 Bomb Disposal Company. Having successfully uplifted the bomb, the crew proceeded to Whitley Common where the device would be detonated with a controlled explosion. While manhandling the bomb off their truck at the common, it exploded, killing seven troops:

Second Lieutenant Alexander Fraser Campbell (42), from Ayrshire
Sergeant Michael Gibson (34)
Sapper William Gibson (22), from Burnage, Lancashire
Sapper Richard Gilchrist (23), from Gorton, Manchester
Sapper Jack Plumb (25)
Sapper Ronald William Skelton (20), from Grange Town, Cardiff
Driver Ernest Frederick George Taylor (32), Royal Army Service Corps
All of them were interred in Coventry's London Road Cemetery.

It is, sadly, with some irony, that two of the men would posthumously be awarded the George Cross, but not for the incident that claimed their lives. Both awards appeared in *The London Gazette* of 21 January 1941.

Second Lieutenant Campbell, the day before he was killed, was called out to deal with an unexploded bomb in the Triumph Engineering Company's works in Coventry. The bomb had halted war production in two factories involving over 1,000 workers and caused the evacuation of local residents. Campbell found it to be fitted with a delayed-action fuse that was impossible to remove. He then made the decision to relocate the bomb to a safe place. This was done by truck, Campbell lying alongside the bomb to enable him to hear if it started ticking so that he could warn the driver. He successfully disposed of it. Campbell's citation was for 'most conspicuous gallantry in carrying out hazardous work in a very brave manner'.

Sergeant Gibson's award was for his actions on 14 September 1940, when duty required him to deal with a large unexploded bomb which had fallen on a factory in the city. While supervising the excavation of the bomb, another exploded nearby. Undaunted, Gibson continued to work on his bomb until it was eventually uncovered. At this time, an 'unusual hissing noise' was heard emanating from the bomb. Gibson immediately sent his men away while he successfully defused the bomb alone. His actions, also described as being of the most conspicuous gallantry, prevented a horrific outcome.

The George Cross.
(Photo MoD)

Dornier Do 17 over the Whittle Arch, Hales Street. (Photo Bundesarchiv and Wikimedia)

19–20 OCTOBER 1940

At lunchtime on Saturday, 19 October, a Luftwaffe pilot brazenly dropped out of the clouds over Coventry and, flitting in between barrage balloon cables at low level, machine-gunned workers who were leaving the Standard Motor Works next to Hearsall Common.

Apparently failing to notice Modern Machine Tools half a mile north of Standard Motor, the German pilot espied a lone car travelling north on Dulverton Avenue, which he promptly decided to strafe with his machine guns. Blissfully oblivious to the impending danger sweeping down on him from behind, estate agent Mr Jordan's reverie was rudely disrupted by the rattle of stones smacking into the underside of his car while plumes of dust erupted next to him. Realizing that he was actually being fired on, Jordan called out to women on the road to take cover. A short while later, Jordan inspected the rear of his car, to find a bullet hole below the rear windscreen. He dug the bullet out and kept it as a souvenir to remind him of the visiting card from one of Hitler's agents!

The Dornier continued northwards before dumping a number of small bombs on a residential estate in the Coundon area. There were no casualties and a gas mains was struck and ignited. With a final burst of machine-gun fire directed at an AFS station, the pilot lifted the Dornier's nose and disappeared back into the clouds.

Coventry work's manager, Ernest William Hancock, was appointed to be an additional Member of the Civil Division of the Most Excellent Order of the British Empire (MBE), for his exemplary leadership during a raid, as reflected in his citation:

A direct hit at Armstrong Siddeley. (Photo courtesy © Rolls Royce Heritage Trust, Derby)

Immediately after an air raid started, Mr Hancock came into the Works, from outside the town, and took charge of all operations. His conduct and leadership were an example to everyone and contributed in no small measure to the excellent work carried out by all concerned.

The Works suffered severely from a number of H.E. and incendiary bombs but in spite of shortage of water all fires when not extinguished quickly, were prevented from spreading to greater proportions.

Towards the end of the raid he was injured when the A.R.P. central control shelter received a direct hit from an H.E. bomb. He assisted, however, in rescuing his colleagues and endeavoured to carry on with his duties but his injuries made this impossible.

The London Gazette, 31 December 1940

That night, the German bombers returned to carry out a 'violent' raid, reckoned to have been the longest and most intense to date. Characterized by the sole usage of heavy-calibre bombs and fewer incendiaries, Humber/Hillman Motors, Armstrong Siddeley, Ordnance Works and GEC were all hit. Armstrong Siddeley sustained particularly severe damage to machine shops and stores on both sides of the road bridge bisecting the complex to the south of the city centre (following page). One of the works' shelters can be seen along this road. Lasting for almost three hours, the raid yet again exacted destruction to civilian life and property.

Badly damaged roofs at the Armstrong Siddeley Works to the south of the city centre. (Photo courtesy © Rolls Royce Heritage Trust, Derby and Snowmanradio)

(Colour photo Wikimedia)

Not far from the city centre, to the north-east a property on 49 Castle Street took a direct hit from a large high-explosive bomb. Reported as being 'in the industrial quarter of the town', the block of houses collapsed over the cellar, entombing, at the time, an unknown number of people. Even as the bombing activity peaked, rescuers and first-aiders battled through an enormous pile of bricks and timber in an effort to extricate those trapped below. Their efforts, however, proved futile, the Herculean task impossible. Fifteen bodies would later be recovered.

Armstrong Siddeley was repeatedly targeted during the Blitz. (Photos courtesy © Rolls Royce Heritage Trust, Derby and Gerry van Tonder)

To the north in Holbrooks, an Anderson shelter on Hen Lane had taken a direct hit. All seven occupants perished. Two church-roof watchers sustained injuries when chunks of debris from a bomb explosion rained down on the church roof, at the same time making fourteen holes in the roof. Sunday services were held as usual.

A wardens' post and an infant school were badly damaged by high-explosive bombs, while across the city, two elderly people were killed when an unexploded bomb scored a direct hit on their Anderson shelter.

In the city, the driver of a tram, together with his female conductor, repeatedly clambered over spiked railings and fences with buckets of sand to extinguish incendiary fires in a timber yard. The gallant woman immediately offered to help anywhere when the firefighting party arrived. Thereafter, she tirelessly ran errands and brought the team much-needed refreshments during the long night. Successive waves of bombers continued to drop their ordnance on Coventry, but this did not stop the woman from doing her bit.

An official communiqué from the Air Ministry and Ministry of Home Security confirmed the raid, but still did not mention the fact that the target had been Coventry:

The enemy's main attacks during the hours of darkness were directed against the London area and the Midlands. Both commenced soon after dusk. The attack on London ceased in the early hours of this morning, and that on the Midlands lasted rather longer.

In the Midlands, the attack was principally on one town, although bombs were dropped in a number of other districts in the area. Damage was caused to houses, shops and commercial premises and some fires resulted. Some people were killed or injured in these areas.

The Midland Daily Telegraph, Monday, 21 October 1940

In improved weather conditions over the continent on the night of 20 October, the RAF attacked Berlin in what an independent source referred to as the 'most severest of the war'. The raid only ended just before dawn. Meanwhile over the English Midlands, Luftwaffe aircraft were heard flying at high altitude. No bombs fell, so it was believed that the aircraft were on a reconnaissance mission.

19–23 OCTOBER 1940

On that Sunday, the German raiders were back over Coventry, hitting the Armstrong Siddeley works and inflicting further damage to parts of the large, sprawling complex straddling Parkside and Puma Road. From the day raid on 19 October through to the 22nd, the central machine shop, gas turbine erecting shop, transport and despatch shed, and a corner of the staff Sphinx Club sustained damage. Coventry Motor Fittings and Morris Motors were also hit. At the same time, the weekend's fatalities continued to increase. While guiding people to a safe place during the raid, a special constable and two ARP wardens were killed when a bomb detonated in a jetty where they had been sheltering. Elsewhere, an elderly couple was killed when their Anderson shelter took a direct hit. In what had become the longest raid since the bombing of Coventry began, there were further fatalities in residential areas.

Civic Offices, Little Park Street and Earl Street, built between 1974-6. (Photos Ministry of Information and Gerry van Tonder)

The Coventry University Art & Design building now stands where once there was only rubble. (Photos Ministry of Information and Snowmanradio)

Successive raids took place on the Monday and Tuesday. On the Monday large numbers of high-explosive, incendiary and delayed-action bombs fell on the city. In what was described as another heavy raid, it was boastfully – perhaps wishfully – reported that ground defences had kept the German bombers away from their objectives. Considerable damage was, however, inflicted on residential properties and some commercial premises. The cycle of death seemed perpetual: two killed when their Anderson shelter took a direct hit, three killed when a building collapsed on them, trapping another six.

Singer Motors on Canterbury Street and Courtaulds in Foleshill were damaged. Radford School was one of three that were hit. Residential areas continued to suffer the brunt of the onslaught, resulting in further fatalities.

On the Tuesday, the fourth successive night of bombing, and in spite of a high number of heavy-calibre bombs and hundreds of incendiaries being dropped, damage to property was less and there were fewer casualties. A few retail outlets were gutted and houses in residential areas damaged. In one particularly large explosion, the concert room of a men's club was badly damaged when a bomb fell to the rear of the premises. The blast knocked over a brick wall at an adjacent bus stop, at the same time blowing over a double-decker bus parked directly in line of the direction of the powerful blast. A nearby bus and several cars were damaged by flying debris. The explosion also shattered a brick street shelter, but only two of the three occupants at the time sustained minor injuries.

(Photos Ministry of Information and Gerry van Tonder)

Elsewhere, the stalls in an open market were destroyed by fire, while a pedestrian was killed by flying shards of glass from a shop front. At a multi-storey building, an elderly night watchman reacted immediately when incendiaries landed on the roof. When three of the devices crashed through the roof, he sped downstairs to grab a bucket of sand to extinguish one of the fires. Help arrived at this point and the other two fires were doused. In surrounding premises where there was no one on duty, incendiary bombs gutted several buildings.

However, some of the city's historic buildings sustained varying degrees of damage. The Holy Trinity Church had its roof damaged while Sibree Hall on Warwick Road was partially destroyed. Remarkably, Holy Trinity escaped any major structural damage, seen opposite as the centre backdrop to a platoon of troops heading towards Broadgate. The spire of the far less fortunate St Michael's rises behind and to the right.

In Bayley Lane, next to St Michael's, the medieval St Mary's Guildhall (pictured below to the immediate left of the Tudor building) took a direct hit from a high-explosive bomb. Erected in the mid-fourteenth century on part of the site where the city's castle once stood, it became home to the United Guild of the Holy Trinity in 1414. Over the centuries since, it was a venue for important civic functions and royal banquets, hosting monarchs such as Henrys V, VI and VII, and James II. In 1569, Elizabeth I had Mary Queen of Scots incarcerated in the hall for three months. During the English Civil War, it served as an armoury.

(Photos Rob Orland and Gerry van Tonder)

(Photo Gerry van Tonder)

Bayley Lane, with the pre-war undamaged Cathedral on the right. (Photos Rob Orland and Gerry van Tonder)

(Photos Ministry of Information and Gerry van Tonder)

The weathered stone exterior attests to the building's age, standing opposite the doomed St Michael's, shown as it was before the Blitz. In the view from the opposite direction, and past St Mary's Street, the width of Bayley Lane narrows considerably, making it even more miraculous that the guildhall survived the inferno in the cathedral a few feet away (previous page).

The ancient woodwork and windows were damaged in various parts of the building, but the greatest damage was to the oldest structure in the hall, Caesar's Tower. The structure is believed to pre-date St Mary's Guildhall and, unusually for a medieval castle tower, was wedge-shaped, not square. Originally comprising four storeys topped with defensive crenulations, in the latter half of the fifteenth century, repair work was undertaken on the tower, suggesting that it had starting falling apart. All that is left today of the twelfth-century castle, and therefore the original eleventh-century Coventry castle, is a section that is now part of the guildhall.

25–30 OCTOBER 1940

After a few relatively quiet days, there were widespread raids in the Midlands during the night of Friday, 25 October. Successive waves of German bombers raided Coventry, starting fires that caused significant damage to residential property, shops and commercial buildings. The first wave dropped incendiaries to light the way for the main attack.

Three occupants of a car were killed when a bomb fell next to a bank as they were driving past. In a cinema, a show was in progress when the raid commenced. Showing great foresight, the manager had his patrons move to seats under the balcony. Moments later, a bomb fell through the cinema's roof. There were fatalities and several badly injured. Elsewhere, a whole family perished when their Anderson shelter took a direct hit. In a property opposite, rescue workers recovered two bodies.

That Saturday, Coventry endured a further two raids: the first with high-explosive bombs, the second with incendiaries. Casualties were lighter than as of late. In its report for the day, the *Telegraph*, tongue in cheek, reported on a 'military objective struck by a Nazi fire-bomb' when a one-man business was hit. Army veteran John Bullock was found standing in the wreckage of his boot-repair shop that he had built up over almost eight years, assessing the damage to machinery and stock. He briefly commented, 'I'm going to keep smiling, and be grim and gay.'

The spires of Holy Trinity, left, and the Cathedral survived the Blitz. (Photos Rob Orland and Gerry van Tonder)

In the second attack an hour later, high-explosive bombs were dropped. One heavy bomb exploded next to an Anderson shelter, the blast lifting the structure out of the ground. None of the occupants was injured.

Holy Trinity vicar Graham Clitheroe in his delightful account of the Blitz, *Coventry under Fire*, recalls how the air-raid sirens had sounded early that Sunday. It had been a memorable day, as the Coventry Girls' Blue Coat School had held a ceremony in the church to celebrate their 230th anniversary. A couple of hours after the warning sirens, incendiaries fell on the west roof. Fortunately, this coincided with the arrival of Clitheroe's second son, John, who immediately set about the fires with a stirrup pump. A short while later Clitheroe also arrived at the church, only to find that one of the incendiary devices had burned through the lead roof, setting fire to the 'ancient' timbers underneath. The biggest problem that the vicar faced, however, was that the double roof concealed the fire itself. At this stage, he felt that he need professional help, and called the fire brigade. Upon their arrival, Fire Officer Brown and his teams immediately set about removing four sections of the lead roof to access the flames. According to Clitheroe, by 10 p.m. it was all over and his church was safe once more. It cost £40 to repair the damage. The installation of hydrants in the church made access to the nave roof with a hose considerably easier.

The incident that Sunday, which could so readily have been a disaster for Holy Trinity, made Clitheroe decide to relinquish his air-raid warden job at Radford so that he could sleep in the church every night. He would take up his post just as the black-out time was approaching.

(Photo courtesy © Rolls Royce Heritage Trust, Derby)

His curate, Reverend Kenneth Thornton, having lost his home during a previous raid, joined the vicar in the nightly fire-guard vigil. This concept of fire watching would become prevalent throughout the city.

The Luftwaffe bombers continued to hit their 'declared' industrial targets in Coventry, with the objective of destroying the city's war production capabilities. In the bombed-out shop at Armstrong Siddeley (previous page) – machine tools half buried under debris – the entrance to staff shelter No. 60 appears in the centre foreground. Employees can only stand and look on, the scale of the destruction overwhelming.

On the Sunday, the Humber Works also sustained major damage, while the Aylesford Inn was totally demolished. On the night of the 29th, the roof over the nave and the south aisle of St Lawrence's Church in Foleshill was completely destroyed.

1–13 NOVEMBER 1940

In the first half of November 1940, relative calm settled over most areas in the country that had been mercilessly and indiscriminately bombed.

Over Coventry, the stillness was punctuated by daily air-raid sirens sounding, together with the occasional daylight raider. Light-night raids took place on the 1st, 3rd, 7th and 12th, during which bombs fell on Whitley, the London Road Pumping Station – a direct hit – and the Congregational Church.

The city tried as best it could to follow normal daily routines – on the High Street and past the banks onto Broadgate, people go about their business. On the 13th, the Duchess of Gloucester, accompanied by the mayor, Alderman John Moseley, toured bombed areas in

Heinkel He 111 daylight raider. (Photos Bundesarchiv and Gerry van Tonder)

A window into pre-war Broadgate. (Photos Rob Orland and Gerry van Tonder)

the city before spending time with the injured in Coventry and Warwickshire Hospital. Her meeting with Mr and Mrs Oldfield may well have been the most moving, as Mr Oldfield spoke of losing seven members of his own family who, together with five others, were killed when a block of houses in Castle Street was bombed on the night of 19 October.

For the first time, the *Telegraph* openly reported on previous bomb damage, specifically mentioning the damage to 'the best-loved place in all Coventry from the viewpoint of antiquarian interest' – St Mary's Hall. St Michael's was also mentioned as having received damage in a raid.

On a daily basis, Coventry's local press published the black-out times for that night and, ominously for the city in November, the phases of the moon:

Black-out Time
5.46 p.m. to7.45 a.m.
To-morrow 5.45 to 7.56
Moon rises 5.18 p.m., sets 8.17 a.m.
The Midland Daily Telegraph, Thursday, 14 November 1940

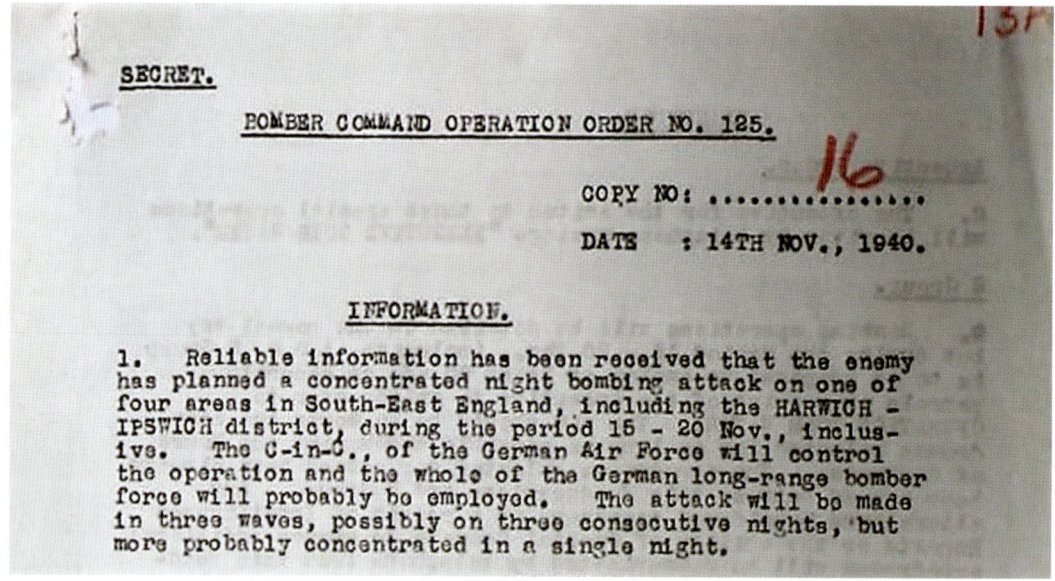

Hours before the apocalypse rained down on Coventry, Bomber Command had totally misinterpreted intelligence about a massive Luftwaffe night raid. (National Archives)

On 11 November, intelligence gleaned from a deciphered German orders' message alerted the Air Ministry to an imminent bombing raid over Britain. In an encrypted order to *Kampfgruppe* 100, a Luftwaffe bomber group based at Vannes in France, new targets were code-listed as 51, 52 and 53, accompanied by X-Gerät radio beam settings. Codenamed *knickebein* – German for crooked leg – it was a system developed by the Germans to allow for target fixing during night-time sorties.

In the 1930s, with the resurgence of Germany's military power, Luftwaffe scientists had already been developing radio navigation systems to facilitate accurate night bombing. Using the short-range, blind-landing Lorenz system, the Germans sought to reverse the fan-shaped radio beams to enable them to converge over a chosen target. Multi-element aerials were devised, with a characteristic 'kink', hence its name. By mid-January, *knickebein* radio-beam transmitters had been erected in Norway, on the German border with Denmark, at Lörrach near the border with France and Switzerland in south-western Germany, in the Netherlands, and in France. *Knickebein*'s Achilles heel was its unsuitability for long-range raids. The X-Gerat apparatus provided the solution. Operating on a much higher frequency, X-Gerät required the manufacture of new radio equipment. In the early stages of trials, limited numbers of radios were made available, so *Kampfgruppe* 100, stationed at Vannes in France, was tasked with guiding the main fleet of bombers over the target. Once a target had been fixed in this manner, marker flares would be deployed for the bombers to home in on. This was the birth of the 'pathfinder' concept, one which, ironically, the RAF would perfect and use against the Germans later in the war.

A code word 'Korn' was also discovered, but, as with the target numbers, interpretation was problematic.

A Luftwaffe pilot, shot down over Britain on the 9th, was overheard boasting to a fellow POW that Göring was planning massive air raids on Britain during the approaching full moon in mid-November. It was subsequently ascertained that the raid had been given the code name *Mondscheinsonate* – Moonlight Sonata. The overall consensus, however, was that London and

Luftwaffe Ju 88 bomber arming for the next sortie. (Photo Bundesarchiv)

German pilots being assisted into their flying gear. (Photo Bundesarchiv)

the south-east would be the main targets. Coventry was only indicated as a possibility. There was, however, no doubt that something big was about to happen over Britain's skies.

Intelligence and reconnaissance sorties conducted over German-occupied France and Belgium reported a marked increase in activity. Bombers, such as the Junkers Ju 88, assembled in dispersal areas, armed and on standby.

The code-breaking scientists at Bletchley Park had run out of time, and it would only be later learned that target 53 was Coventry, codenamed *Korn*. It was generally believed that it would be a large-scale attack, but any specific target remained open to speculation and went unrecorded.

On 12 November, Director of Home Operations (DHO), Air Vice-Marshal Donald Fasken Stevenson OBE, DSO, MC and Bar, addressed a secret minute to the deputy chief of air staff (DCAS), in which he expressed his belief that sufficient intelligence was to hand to formulate a counter-plan to the imminent German's Operation Moonlight Sonata.

Listing thirty-eight Luftwaffe airfields – from Amsterdam in the east to Caen in the west – from which night raids were being launched into Britain, Stevenson selected thirty 'which we shall have to tackle'. He outlined the plan, codenamed Operation Cold Water:

(a) The A.C.A.S. [Assistant Chief of Air Staff] should arrange to bring all his anti-beam stations in throughout the night in order to bend the [*knickebein*] beams and interfere with the beams upon which the enemy scale of attack will operate.

(b) We should tell Fighter Command, and as soon as practicable, give the likely objective and avenues of approach. On these Fighter Command should operate the maximum number of 'cats eye' [Airborne Interception radar, AI] fighters plus what Beaufighters are available. In respect of the Blenheim fighters, this is an excellent opportunity for taking offensive action against enemy bombers.

We should ask C.-in-C. [Commander-in-Chief] to put some Blenheim fighters over the closer aerodromes and to keep them there as long as ammunition lasts with the object of shooting down enemy bombers as they take off. Additionally we should keep some 'cats eyes' and other Hurricanes over Fécamp. We know that the harbour light there has been turned into a beacon and that the JU. 88's and Heinkels on making this light on their return journey, switch on their navigation lights and home to their aerodromes. C.-in-C. Fighter Command will, of course, warn the A.A. [anti-aircraft] Command and we should authorise him, if this is necessary, to allow an extra expenditure of anti-aircraft ammunition for the night in question.

(c) In respect of action by the Bomber Force, we have to consider two things:

(i) Security patrols are obviously necessary and these should be carried out over 30 aerodromes. From No. 1 and 2 Group – even though a large number of Squadrons are rearming with heavies – we should be able to get at least 150 sorties – for an action like this, possibly more, including the Battle Squadrons. The Battle Squadrons could take on the closer objectives, the Blenheims the more distant. We should be careful that the security patrol on this occasion is carried out to best advantage, i.e. the bomber should not arrive and throw its bombs on the aerodrome and come home, but should be armed with the largest number of small bombs possible and stay in the vicinity of the enemy aerodromes as long as possible, throwing a bomb when it is apparent that aircraft are taking off – or at irregular intervals. We could

Bristol Blenheim. (Photo Alan Wilson)

Lancaster on a bombing raid over Germany. (Photo RAF)

also blow up the number of mediums by Coastal Command aircraft. We could probably get an additional 20 to 30 sorties of Blenheims, Albacores and Swordfish. The coastwise aerodromes would be suitable objectives for them.

(ii) The action by the heavy bomber force will require careful consideration. To pour cold water on the Moonlight Sonata we should remember that if the maximum scale of night attack is concentrated on a place like London or Birmingham, no matter what we do, serious superficial damage will be done and high casualties caused – quite apart from any key point that may be hit. In consequence we should remember that the very best way of turning cold water on an operation of this kind from the point of John Citizen is to hit back at a similarly important area in Germany as hard as we can. We suggest that the heavy bomber force, instead of being spread over the aerodromes (additional to the Mediums) should be concentrated in a big bang on either the Ruhr or Berlin. Moreover, we should on this occasion use our 'Jericho Gear'. The whistles for our bombs have already gone out to Depots and there should be no trouble in getting them fitted to our 250 and 500 lb. bombs for an occasion of this kind. If the big bang is to achieve the best moral effect we suggest we do this.

If you were to decide on a choice as between Berlin or the Ruhr this would automatically cut out operations against Italy for perhaps three nights during the high moon period. I am not certain whether you would be willing to do this. With weather conditions as they are at this time of the year it might well mean that we miss an opportunity during the best moon conditions of attacking Italy. Our feeling is that the Whitleys should not be included in the 'cold water' plan but that they should take on Italy with the 'cold water' plan as an alternative for them should weather conditions on that night be unsuitable for operations against Italy.

(iii) In respect of the attack on Vannes Aerodrome from which K.G. 100 work we should delay this until the night on which the 'Cold Water' Plan is put into effect.

The next day, Wednesday, 13 November, Deputy Chief of Air Staff (DCAS), Air Vice-Marshal William Sholto Douglas DFC, MC, responded by informing the DHO that the Chief of Air Staff, Air Chief Marshal Charles Portal DFC, MC, agreed with the proposed plan, adding that the Anti-Aircraft Command should be 'encouraged to move his AA guns to the probable lines of approach', based on known *knickebein* beam routes. He also felt that particular attention should be given to the deployment of 'special' Whitleys to detect river beams on to the beam station at Cherbourg.

Douglas stressed that his superior was 'particularly anxious' that the Luftwaffe *Kampfgruppe* 100 airfield at Vannes in France 'should be severely attacked'. Douglas's instructions were precise and clear: '… get out an Operation Order, putting your proposals, with these additions, into effect, for issue to all concerned. The sooner we can get this out the better.'

In a post script to his missive, Douglas, almost as an afterthought, wrote:

You will note from minute 2 that it is probable that the operation will consist of three attacks to be carried out on three successive nights. We must therefore be prepared to repeat our 'Cold-Weather' [sic] Plan on three successive nights, although personally I very much doubt whether the enemy will get three successive nights of fine weather.

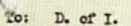

To: D. of I.

From: S/L S.D. Felkin.

Date: 12.11.1940.

A pilot from 2/K.G. 1 from MONDIDIER shot down on the 9th inst. has told the following story to his roommate. (A S.P. installed two days ago [if this isn't clear Group Captain Davidson will explain].) He believes that riots have broken out in London and that Buckingham palace has been stormed and that 'Hermann' thinks the psychological moment has come for a colossal raid to take place between the 15th and the 20th of this month at the full moon and that Coventry and Birmingham will be the towns attacked. P/W stated he had recently made 2 to 3 attacks on London nightly but that this attack will only entail one flight per night and that every bomber in the Luftwaffe will take part. He says that workmen's dwellings are being concentrated on methodically in order to undermine the working classes who are believed to be so near revolt. He thinks that every Knickebein route will be employed and that in future they will concentrate on 50 kg shreiking bombs.

As this came after S/L Humphrey's visit this afternoon when he mentioned that a gigantic raid under the code name of "Moonlight sonata" was in preparation, I thought it well to bring this information to your notice although on account of the source it should be treated with reserve.

With only two days to go to the big raid on Coventry, British intelligence was no closer to understanding what lay in the immediate future. (National Archives)

Later that same day, Douglas received a 'Most Secret' minute from the DHO stating that the 'same source' of intelligence (the German PoW) had indicated at 7 p.m. that there would be a code word for each day or phase of the impending German operation, Moonlight Sonata:

First day or phase   REGENSCHIRM (umbrella)
Second day or phase   MONDSCHEIN SERENADE (Moonshine Serenade)
Third day or phase   Not known
You will note that the code word for the second day is somewhat like code name for the general operation – Moonlight Sonata.

In his own writing, Douglas wrote directly on the latest message:

D.H.O.
To see. I really can't believe that this is a three night show. I believe these are three phases. 'Umbrella' is K.G. 100. 'Moonshine Serenade' is the main attack. No. 3 phase is something else. How can even the optimistic Boche hope to get 3 successive nights of fine weather
    Please raise at my meeting tomorrow morning.

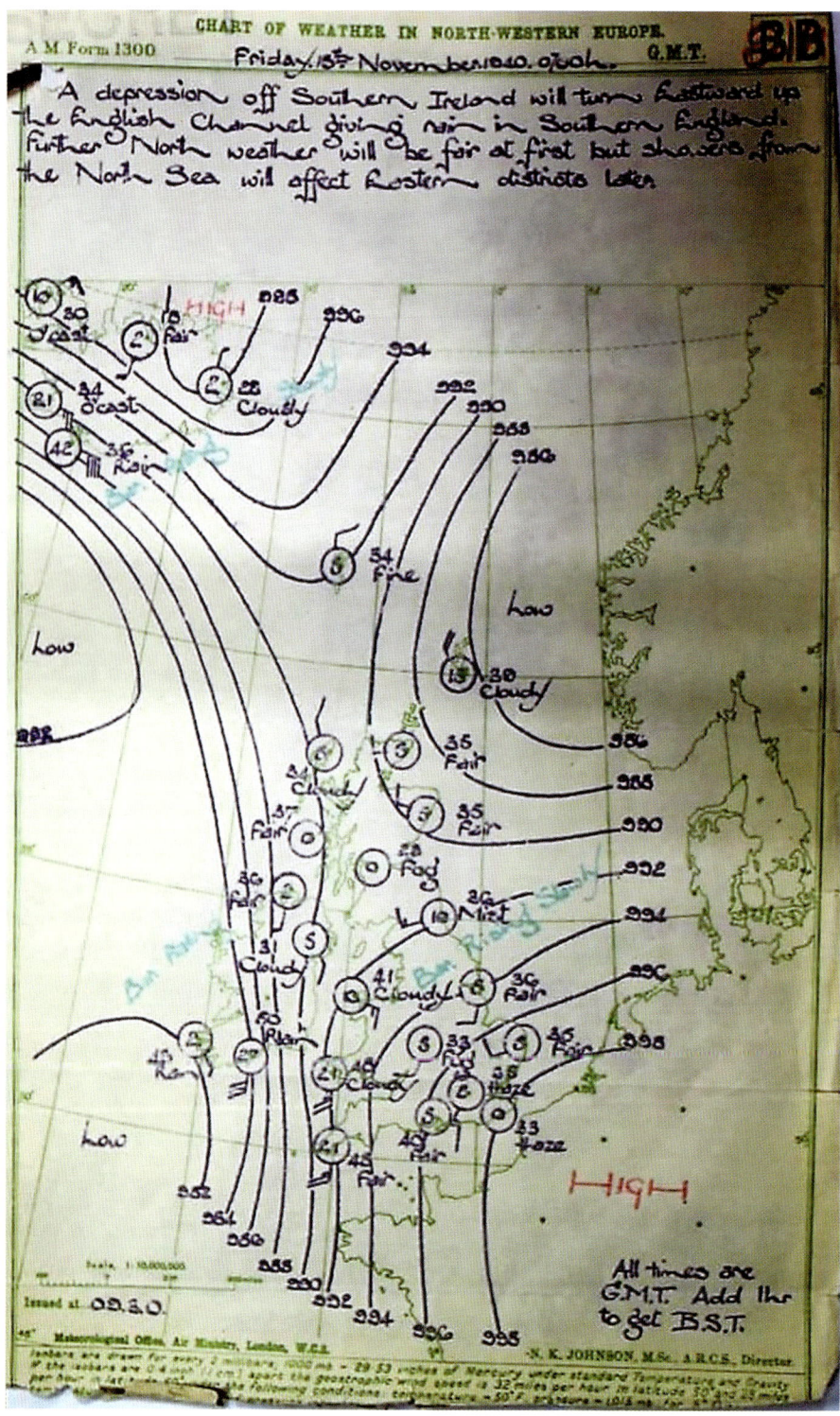

The weather chart at the time from the Air Ministry's Meteorological Office. (National Archives)

Bofors anti-aircraft gun and crew. (Photos Ministry of Information and Gerry van Tonder)

'Tomorrow morning' would be 14 November 1940. Final confirmation of the Luftwaffe's intended target in Britain remained uncertain. To the north, is was just another routine day for Coventry's air defences, the four-man crews of the 40mm Bofors conducting drills to ensure they remained efficient (depicted above).

A one-page record of the meeting was also written by hand, this time by DHO Stevenson. There were three terse points, each only a sentence long:

Note.
CAS
Vice-CAS
DCAS
Informed that
(a)   the operation order was made on the assumption that M-sonata would be in three phases on a single night;
(b)   the Fighter [cover] of enemy bombers over their aerodromes was dropped as it would have to be taken from out of a Blenheim Squadron;
(c)   The 4 Target areas only were indicated in the Order, & not Birmingham and Coventry.
CAS agreed.

Stevenson immediately followed this up with an operation order to the RAF duty group captain. Also passing on the file on Cold Water, the DHO instructed that the receipt of an enemy calibration signal would indicate that Moonlight Sonata would take place that day.

A telegram template (pictured below) was attached for the RAF duty officer to disseminate as soon as he received this information. Thereafter, intelligence from Wing Commander Grant would be received, confirming target-selection areas and the German beams that had been activated, together with their direction and point of intersection. A second telegram should then be sent to the various listed commands to enable them to 'deduce' the area that would be under attack and the flight paths on which the enemy bombers would be approaching the target or targets. The RAF chiefs and the DHO would then be informed that Cold Water was on.

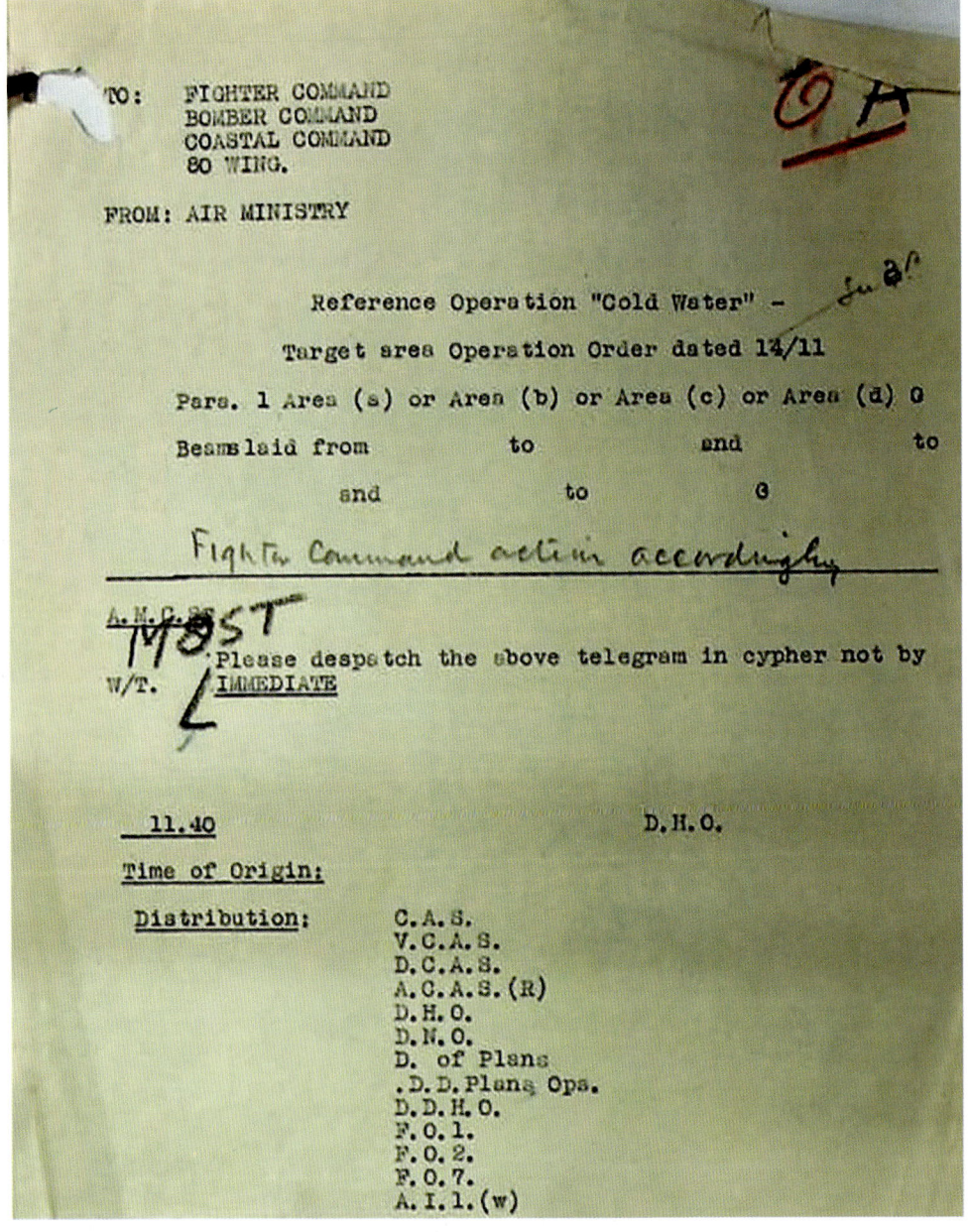

(National Archives)

In a Most Secret 'note', it was confirmed that, 'by 1500 hours on the 14th November', the Radio Counter-measures Organisation was able to report that the enemy 'River Group' beams were intersecting over Coventry.

As the anticipated sequence of events started unfolding, Stevenson scribbled a brief note of confirmation on the file copy of the duty group captain's orders:

14.11.40
Note
The 1300 hrs signal was made today and acknowledged by [Luftwaffe] HQ Air Fleet 3. C.A.S. decided to go ahead with 'Cold Water' and spoke to Commands and issued instructions at 1615 hrs.
14/11
D.F. Stevenson
D.H.O.

As a quick rider, Stevenson wrote, 'Would you please be prepared to act tonight.'

el.

MOST SECRET

NOTE FOR THE PRIME MINISTER ON PROJECTED OPERATION BY G.A.F. – "MOONLIGHT SONATA" AND THE COUNTER OPERATION BY THE METROPOLITAN AIR FORCE – "COLD WATER"

From a good source of information we learn that the enemy propose to carry out a heavy night bombing attack on targets in an area in this country. The areas, which are probably alternative to each other, are Central London (not absolutely definite), Greater London, the area bounded by Farnborough – Maidenhead – Reading and the area bounded by Rochester – Favisham – Isle of Sheppey. The areas are apparently alternative and the selection would be on the point of weather or visibility.

2. The whole of the German long range Bomber Force will be employed. The operation is being co-ordinated, we think, by the Commander-in-Chief, G.A.F. It is probably a reprisal for our attack on Munich. K.G.100, led in person by the Geschwader Commander, will carry out the first phase of the operation and the first attacks.

3. The attack will probably take place on a night between 15th and 20th of November, i.e. during the full moon period. At 13.00 hours on the day preceding the night on which the attack is to be launched, K.G.100 (the experts of knickebein type radio navigation) will carry out a reconnaissance over the target areas to discover whether the intersection of the beams is in fact over the selected objective and at this time will transmit a weather report, which will be replied to by Air Fleet Headquarters. This will be our signal that the party is on.

Informing Churchill. (National Archives)

(Photos Ministry of Information and Gerry van Tonder)

Prime Minister Churchill was also given a comprehensive report on both operations: Moonlight Sonata and Cold Water. The document is liberally laced with the word 'probably', reflecting the Air Ministry's uncertainty as to where the Luftwaffe would strike.

In a little over three hours, the first bombs would fall on Coventry.

At 4 p.m. the next day, Friday, 15 November, Fighter Command received a memo from the Air Ministry, instructing two Whitley aircraft of 80 Wing to conduct staggered bombing attacks against German beam transmitters at Cherbourg on the French coast. By this time, Coventry was already in ruins, a fact that they would have known about.

Thirty minutes before the Luftwaffe unleashed a firestorm on an unsuspecting Coventry, the city received the first warning that they were about to be bombed. By this time, around ten pathfinder Heinkel He 111 bombers from Vannes had long since crossed the Channel and were closing in on the city.

14–15 NOVEMBER 1940 'MOONLIGHT SONATA'

Air-raid sirens wailed across the city, shelter was sought, and ARP wardens walked the streets, spreading the alert and ensuring compliance with air-raid protocol. On occasion this might have entailed the warden kitting himself out in gas-protection gear, then walking through the streets whirring a wooden rattle as a warning of a possible gas attack (pictured above). On the left, two Coventry historians take in the situation: Rob Orland, left, looking at the sky above

Council House, while Dave McGrory watches the warden striding towards Bayley Lane and St Michael's Cathedral. (See acknowledgements at the end of the book.)

At 7.40 p.m., the Heinkel He 111 vanguard dropped more than 10,000 incendiaries and around 50 SC50 bombs on Coventry.

The fire services were immediately inundated with calls to attend to dozens of fires created by the incendiaries. Ruptured gas mains lit up the cold night sky, creating target beacons for the next wave of bombers. Their job successfully completed, shortly after 8 p.m., the Heinkels disappeared into the dark.

Fifteen minutes later, the main raid was initiated by a flight of Heinkels dropping high-explosive and incendiary bombs, and landmines. Flying to a well-executed pattern, every fifteen minutes thereafter flights of about twenty Heinkels, Dornier Do 17s and Junker Ju 88s each, flew over the city from five different directions, dropping an enormous amount and type of ordnance.

Just after 6 a.m., the all-clear sounded, heralding the end of the first nightmare. Massed squadrons, numbering over 500 bombers, had left France that night to execute Operation

Heinkel over Coventry. (Photos Bundesarchiv and dorvak/jonn)

The National Provincial Bank (today NatWest) building portico miraculously escaped damage. (Photos David McGrory and Gerry van Tonder)

Unexploded German ordnance in front of Holy Trinity. (Photos Ministry of Information and Gerry van Tonder)

St Michael's reduced to a shell. (Photos Rob Orland and Gerry van Tonder)

Moonlight Sonata. Splitting off from the main group, forty-odd aircraft headed for London to create a diversion and to drop mines into the Thames.

Locking in on Coventry, individual flights from the flotilla lined up on their respective pre-arranged bombing runs. Over the next eleven hours, the punishingly incessant waves of bombers, flying at between 20–30,000 feet, dropped 30,000 incendiaries, 50 parachute-guided landmines, 64 flarebombs and 500 tons of high-explosive and oil bombs. It was not uncommon for the massive landmines to fail to detonate, possibly due to slowness of descent. Such devices posed a perilous threat to the police and emergency services.

On the 15th, the British printed media headlined the tragedy that had just befallen Coventry. The nation was shocked.

NAZI 'TERROR' RAID ON COVENTRY
Random Bombing: Casualties Feared Nearly 1,000
  Cathedral Among Many Buildings Destroyed
   The city of Coventry was heavily attacked by Nazi bombers last night and the number of casualties may be in the neighbourhood of 1,000, the Ministry of Home Security announced today.

It is feared that extensive damage was done and many buildings were destroyed, including the Cathedral.

The raiders were heavily engaged by intensive A.A. fire which kept them at a great height and hindered the accurate bombing of industrial targets, but the city itself suffered seriously.

Indiscriminate Bombing

The attack was begun by scattering incendiary bombs over a wide area. Fires broke out at many points and the indiscriminate bombardment of whole city followed.

The scale of the raids was comparable to the largest night attacks on London.

'Reprisal Raid,' Says Berlin

The attacks on Coventry are described by the Berlin wireless as reprisals for the abortive raids of the R.A.F. on Munich on the night of November 8.

Numerous bombs of the largest calibre were dropped on the armament works, it is stated, and it is added that as early as 8 p.m. (B.S.T.) over 20 fires were visible in Coventry, illuminating the way for further German bombers which attacked in successive waves.

The fires, the Germans claim, spread and destroyed not only buildings and machinery, but also large quantities of raw material and finished products.

Nazi officials say that last night's attacks on Coventry were 'the greatest in the history of air warfare.'

Liverpool Evening Express, Friday, 15 November 1940

Casualties in the city were catastrophic: 568 killed, 863 seriously injured, many with life-threatening wounds, and 343 with relatively minor injuries. In addition to schools, clubs, shops, business premises and pubs, 2,300 homes were demolished. A further 29,000 were damaged and 5,600 declared unsafe to live in. St Michael's Cathedral was reduced to a roofless shell.

The fact that, on the morning of the 15th, the 'heaviest raid of the war' on Berlin had grabbed the *Telegraph*'s front-page headline, would have been by design and not simply by coincidence. RAF bombers had also made the most of the full moon to stage their own sonata. This time, however, there was no reference to 'a Midlands town'. What had happened to Coventry during the night could no longer be hushed up for propaganda reasons. A communiqué from the Ministry of Home Security issued in the afternoon was unequivocally clear: 'The City of Coventry was heavily attacked last night ... the scale of the raids was comparable with those of the largest night attacks on London.'

Condemnation from Britain's allies, especially the United States press, was powerful and uncompromising:

U.S. PRESS CONDEMNS COVENTRY BOMBING

'The Nazi air-raid on Coventry, which reduced a great part of the Midlands city to debris, is Hitler's most ruthless act of indiscriminate warfare since the Battle of Britain began,' says the *St. Louis Global Democrat*.

'The smouldering ruins of Coventry are new evidence that the Nazi war machine has stripped the last tenuous shred of civilisation from modern warfare.'

The *Cleveland Plain Dealer* writes: 'Hitler raises horror to the superlative. There is not room enough in the 20th Century world for the author of Coventry's sorrow and for decent men at the same time'.

'Barbarity becomes too tame a word as the gibbering Nazi propaganda swirls around the ruins, shrieking that this is their leader's vengeance,' says the *New York Herald Tribune* in a leading article on the Coventry air raid.

Factory damage along Parkside. (Photos courtesy © Rolls Royce Heritage Trust, Derby and Gerry van Tonder)

'For the sick and helpless which such a spectacle evokes there is but one answer. No means of defence which the United States can place in British hands should be withheld, no effort which this country and every individual can make to stop this horror while still confined beyond the seas is too great to make.

'So long as Britain stands, a Coventry anywhere in the United States is all but impossible, but only so long. Our own front line is above such ruins as those of Coventry or London, and that line must be held if any aid that we can send will hold it.'

The Midland Daily Telegraph, Monday, 18 November 1940

On the morning of the 15th, a first secret report was compiled on the Coventry Blitz that had taken place during the night:

First Report on Enemy Operation 'Moonlight Sonata'
Reports up to 0700 hours show that approximately 360 enemy sorties have been directed at Coventry. The attack was started by special aircraft of K.G. 100 on the 'River' group beams. The attack started at about 1900 hours and finished at about 0600 hours.

A large number of fires have been started and many key points damaged. All the fire fighting facilities within Coventry had been brought into action by 2130 hours, and assistance was sent from Oxford, Banbury, Aylesbury and Rugby. Control of the fire fighting services has been moved from Coventry to the standby control at Rugby.

Amongst the vital points hit is the Post Office Exchange which has been abandoned. As a result communications have been seriously affected.

Coventry's air defences, such as this 3.7in. anti-aircraft gun, were ineffective. (Photos Gerry van Tonder)

The gun operations room at Coventry was hit but at 0635 hours was still controlling all the guns in the defended area, with the exception of six. No casualties to guns or personnel are reported and so far as is known all guns remained in action throughout the operation.

A message at 0636 hours from Balloon Command stated that so far as was known the Balloon Barrage was maintained all night. Communication with the Coventry balloon barrage squadrons was however cut. A despatch rider was being sent in to find out the latest information.

Up to midnight a total of 54 fighter sorties had been sent up. 4 interceptions have been reported of which two resulted in combats which were, however, indecisive. Fighter patrols were maintained over Coventry by Blenheim fighters during the following periods:

1857 hours to 2114 hours

0136 hours to 0336 hours

0140 hours to 0340 hours

0440 hours until enemy clear of Coventry.

Bomber Command's effort during the night amounted to 122 aircraft of which 49 were directed on Berlin, 53 on enemy aerodromes, 17 on the Hamburg oil refineries, and 3 on mine laying. Security patrols on aerodromes report good success with fires and explosions. First reports of the Berlin Operation state that large fires were started which could be seen from a considerable distance.

Hawker Hurricanes and a Supermarine Spitfires provided air defence. (Photos Ronnie Macdonald and Gerry van Tonder)

An unidentified RAF group captain authored a second report under secret cover:

Report on Enemy Operation 'Moonlight Sonata'

1. With reference to the First Report on the abovementioned enemy operation it is now confirmed that the number of sorties which operated against COVENTRY was 300.
2. The following additional factories which sustained damage have been added to the list [not found]:
   Messrs. Courtaulds Ltd.
   Sterling Metals Ltd.
   Herbert Alfred Ltd. (completely gutted)
3. Amongst other buildings damaged are the Cathedral, the General Post Office, the Central Police Station and hospitals. Gas, water and electrical services within the city are practically at a standstill.
4. The number of casualties has not yet been ascertained, but it is stated to be in the region of 600.
5. It is confirmed that the Balloon Barrage was maintained all night. I am informed by Balloon Command that as far as they are able to ascertain, in view of cut communications, casualties are slight.
6. It has now been ascertained that 114 fighter sorties were sent up, but there have been no confirmed reports of interceptions.

A University of Coventry building on one of the former Armstrong Siddeley sites. (Photos courtesy © Rolls Royce Heritage Trust, Derby and Gerry van Tonder)

WIDE WORLD PHOTOS : PLEASE WATCH CREDIT
935693
    SCENE OF DEVASTATING GERMAN AERIAL ATTACK

COVENTRY, ENGLAND- AN AERIAL VIEW OF THE ANCIENT CITY
OF COVENTRY, WHERE CASUALTIES ARE CLOSE TO A THOUSAND
AND PROPERTY DAMAGE IS TREMENDOUS, FOLLOWING WHAT THE
NAZIS DESCRIBE AS "THE GREATEST ATTACKS IN THE HISTORY
OF AERIAL WARFARE" LAST NIGHT. FOR 10 AND 1/2 HOURS
GERMAN BOMBERS ROARED OVER THE CITY, JUST 85 MILES
NORTHWEST OF LONDON, SUBJECTING THE POPULATION OF
167.90 THE GREATEST TERROR THEY HAD EVER KNOWN.
EXTENSIVE DAMAGE WAS DONE AND MANY BUILDINGS WERE
DESTROYED, INCLUDING THE COVENTRY CATHEDRAL, WHOSE
FAMOUS STEEPLE RISES 303 FEET, AND SEEN IN THE RIGHT
BACKGROUND, ABOVE. GERMAN INFORMANTS SAID THE RAID
WAS IN RETALIATION FOR THE BRITISH ATTACK ON MUNICH
WHERE HITLER SPOKE AT A NAZI PARTY CELEBRATION A
WEEK AGO.

              O-11/15/40 (S)

Press release. (Photo Rob Orland)

At the Deputy Chief of the Air Services' conference held on the 15th, it was agreed that it would serve no purpose in 'withholding publication of the fact that Coventry was the target of last night's enemy operations, but that D.P.R. should ensure that reports of damage are "damped down" as much as possible'.

With the stunned city still taking stock of the night-time disaster, published references to the raids spoke of the raids in broad terms only: 'It is feared that extensive damage was done and many buildings destroyed, including the Cathedral ... the number of casualties may be in the neighbourhood of a thousand ... the people of Coventry bore their ordeal with great courage'.

The following day, King George VI visited Coventry where, over a period of four hours, he covered vast bombed areas on foot, even to the extent of clambering over debris. Disclosing that it was his own wish to come, the monarch shared the city's grief, offering gratitude and encouragement to emergency services and civilians alike.

The Parliamentary Secretary to the Ministry of Health, Florence Horsbrugh, spent the night in Coventry to personally oversee arrangements for the welfare of those who, in one night of misery, had become homeless. By early evening on the Friday, food and rest centres had been opened in neighbouring Warwickshire, Worcestershire, Leicestershire and Northamptonshire to receive the refugees. Buses were laid on to accomplish this task, as well as to evacuate air-raid casualties and the very ill and aged.

Coventry ARP Controller, Captain A. S. Hector, said of the city's mood, 'There is not the slightest sign of panic here.'

The Royal party in the ruins of the Cathedral. (Photos Rob Orland and Gerry van Tonder)

The debris-filled shell of St Michael's. (Photos Rob Orland and Gerry van Tonder)

The risk of contracting serious diseases from contaminated water was extremely high, resulting in a sustained campaign by the Coventry health authorities, encouraging the city's population to be inoculated:

CITY OF COVENTRY
Prevention of Typhoid Fever
In view of the present damage to drainage communications in the City, special precautions against typhoid are advised.
  Boil all drinking water and milk.
  Seek personal protection by inoculation.
If you want to be INOCULATED, go to one of the following centres between 10 a.m. and 12 noon:
    1. The Joint Laboratory at Coventry and Warwickshire Hospital.
    2. City Isolation Hospital, Whitley.
    3. Gulson Road First Aid Post.

A. Massey, M.D.
Medical Officer of Health
The Council House, Coventry

On 17 November, the Air Ministry drew up a military synopsis and post mortem report of the events of the 14th. Detailing apparent successes of the RAF against Luftwaffe forward airfields

Homeless ... often orphaned. (Photos New Times Paris Bureau Collection and Snowmanradio)

in France and over selected targets in Germany, the deputy director of home operations took stock of the efficacy – or lack of – by Coventry's defences that night:

A total of 121 fighter sorties were despatched during the night, consisting of 10 A.I. [Airborne Interception radar] Beaufighters, 39 A.I. Blenheims, 22 Defiants, 45 Hurricanes, 4 Gladiators and 2 Spitfires. The fighter operations resulted in 11 A.I. detections, culminating in one enemy sighting: one sighting by searchlights and 9 unassisted sightings. 2 engagements resulted from these sightings and one enemy aircraft was damaged.

The disappointing number of combats which followed on the 21 interceptions or enemy detections is attributed, inter alia, to the exhaust glow from Hurricanes and [Boulton] Defiants, which has the double disability of interfering with the pilot's vision and acting as a warning beacon to enemy bombers. The poor vision through the Perspex screens of Blenheims and Hurricanes is also a contributory excuse.

The fighter deployment provided for patrols over the target area, patrols across the beams and on enemy lines of approach, and also for vectoring on to specific enemy raiders.

The Coventry barrage of 56 balloons was reinforced on the 14th November by 16 further balloons, 8 of which were deployed on the night 14–15th. The Barrage was flying throughout the enemy attack, and no enemy aircraft came below the level of the balloons. Balloon casualties resulting from the bombardment were slight.

40 high angle [anti-aircraft] guns were deployed for the defence of Coventry, and these remained in action throughout the bombardment. Although the Gun Operations Room was bombed it soon returned to action, and at the end of the operation was in control of all the heavy [3.7in] anti-aircraft except for 6 guns.

The light anti-aircraft deployed in Coventry had been increased on the 12th November by 12 [40mm] Bofors provided by Home Forces.

It is estimated that some 330 enemy aircraft were engaged in the attack on Coventry, which was opened by some 10 aeroplanes of KG-100, which flew up the beams and started fires in the target area. The remaining aircraft then bombed the fires. While earlier raids followed the beams they were soon abandoned by subsequent sorties, which took full advantage of the bright moonlight and approached the objective over a wide front.

Air chiefs and the Air Ministry demanded full explanations as to how massed German bombers had been able to pulverize Coventry the whole night with virtual impunity, with both ground and air defences failing to even hinder the endless waves of enemy bombers over the city, let alone account for a single one.

Be that as it may, the strength of the attack was overwhelming, coming as it did along five corridors of different altitudes in an east–south ninety-degree arc from France, Belgium and the Netherlands. There was only one target. After the raid, the bombers exited for home in only two directions: directly east and directly south.

The Air Ministry conducted its own estimate of the initial stages of the raid, based on German targeting radio beams, beacons, points of origin and known Luftwaffe *kampfgruppen* compositions and strengths at those bases. The Luftwaffe front facing Britain across the English Channel was 465 miles wide.

Extensive destruction at the Armstrong Siddeley works south of the city. (Photos Ministry of Information and Gerry van Tonder)

Between 1910–1930
10 raids Cherbourg–Bristol–Coventry
Between 1950–2020
6 raids Isle of White–Coventry
6 raids The Wash–Coventry
Between 2030–2050
18 raids Isle of Wight–Coventry
18 raids Great Yarmouth–Coventry
Between 2050–2130
16 raids Great Yarmouth–Coventry
14 raids Kent–Coventry
Between 2130–2155
10 raids East Coast–Coventry
14 raids Dieppe–London–Coventry
At 2155
16 raids Beachy Head–London–Coventry
3 raids The Wash–Coventry

By the 20th, amidst a massive repair, restoration and clean-up exercise of Biblical proportions, individual accounts of the night of the raid started trickling in.

For Holy Trinity Church, weeks of rooftop vigilance and preparation by her clergy had paid dividends. That evening, as was their routine, the vicar, Reverend Graham Clitheroe, and his curate, Reverend Kenneth Thornton, drew the black-out curtains. After checking on their 100-gallon stock of water, stored in the church in dolly tubs and buckets, the two clergymen dutifully took up their posts in the North Porch vestry.

The raid began with a 'shower' of incendiaries to the north of Holy Trinity, and even at this early stage, Clitheroe felt that the raid was 'strangely persistent'. While commenting to his colleague that the developing scene around them was one of 'dramatic intensity', an incendiary fell through the roof of the church's Marler Chapel, starting a fire on the roof in the process.

It took the two men operating a stirrup pump less than five minutes to douse the fires.

They then took to the roof to assess the situation. What they could see of the city shocked them. It seemed that every building was ablaze. From the solid crump of exploding bombs, they knew that the Germans were dropping heavy-calibre, high-explosive bombs.

Crossing over to the east roof, they saw with trepidation that several incendiaries had fallen on the roof of St Michael's, Holy Trinity's close neighbour. As they stood watching helplessly, and knowing that they could not desert Holy Trinity, the fires in the cathedral's roof were spreading rapidly. It became evident to Clitheroe that St Michael's provost, Basil White, and his two-man team would not be able to contain the blaze.

No high-explosive bombs had struck St Michael's. The intense heat of the incendiaries had melted holes in the outer lead roof, allowing the devices to drop onto the beams of the underlying roof. The fire brigade was spread thinly throughout the city centre, totally overwhelmed by the magnitude of the firestorm, while facing a dwindling supply of water. Vividly recalling the vista later, Clitheroe wrote, 'It was a hateful sight to watch this glorious edifice, so cared for through the long centuries by the Church, being eaten up by the fire of enemy bombs – hateful as it was senseless … the Cathedral was doomed'.

Holy Trinity did not meet the same fate as St Michael's. (Photos David McGrory and Gerry van Tonder)

Holy Trinity spire. (Photo Gerry van Tonder)

Holy Trinity and, to the right, the Cathedral spire. (Photo Gerry van Tonder)

(Photos Ministry of Information and Gerry van Tonder)

Numb with emotion, Clitheroe and Thornton returned to the nave, where they were faced with more tragedy: the City Library, adjacent to Holy Trinity's southern boundary wall, was aflame. A repository of priceless historical records, Clitheroe knew that they were powerless to do anything, later writing, 'nothing on earth could have saved Coventry Library.' In the light of day, Holy Trinity stands over debris from the library (depicted above). The Coventry Cross is a twentieth-century addition.

Founded in 1873 by former mayor, John Gulson, the Free Library once stood on the narrow lane opposite Holy Trinity and towards the cathedral. Although sustaining severe damage during the Blitz, the library was rebuilt.

At that moment, a second incendiary device fell into Holy Trinity's Archdeacon's Court, perhaps providing the church's shattered clergy a distraction from the apocalyptic destruction that they were witnessing around them. The vicar, with full justification, would liken it to 'Dante's Inferno'.

Having placed buckets of sand and water, stirrup pumps, axes and spades at strategic points inside the cathedral and the various roofs, St Michael's fire-guard team carried out regular drills to hone the actions they would have to take should the cathedral get bombed. After the relatively minor roof fires on 14 October, the men knew that the removal of sheets of lead to access fires on the timbers 18in below would be a major challenge. Stonemason Jock Forbes, on duty the whole night, had an intimate knowledge of the cathedral's layout. The other three members of the guard that night were drawn from the regular team of Messrs J. Gratwick of Armstrong Siddeley, W. H. Eaton of Smith's Stamping, and Lane. Messrs Wright, Robson, Lowrie, Harling, Wells, Brums and Turner were volunteers from the YMCA, while Reverend R. A. Edwards and the church provost, Dick Howard, completed the team.

The City Library destroyed in the Blitz, as it once stood in the shadow of the Cathedral's spire. (Photos Rob Orland and Gerry van Tonder)

At 7 p.m. on 14 November, Forbes was joined by Eaton, Wright and the provost as they assembled on the roof of the nave. It was a cold, still night, awash with moonlight. A raid was expected. Soon after the warning siren had broken the silence, the unmistakeable laboured drone of fully armed bombers could be heard. The fire-guard team crouched down just below roof level on the stone staircase that wound down to the north aisle below.

Peering towards the now glowing horizon, the men could see the detonating incendiaries edging ever closer to the cathedral, accompanied by the characteristic loud bang as each device exploded a minute after igniting.

At around 7.40 p.m., the first incendiary hit St Michael's, falling on the eastern section of roof over the chancel. A second device penetrated both levels of roof, landing on the nave floor near the pulpit. Yet another fell on the south aisle roof above the organ, searing through the lead and landing on top of the oak timbers below. This was what the guard had feared most, as the spot was very difficult to access. All four men hacked away at the lead sheeting until they had made a large enough hole through which to pour buckets of sand, simultaneously stirrup-pumping bucket upon bucket of water through the cavity. Eventually they brought the fire under control, but a short distance from where they were toiling smoke start billowing out from under another section of the lead roof.

Like clocks that stopped on the night that St Michael's Cathedral was destroyed by an inferno of intense heat created by German incendiary bombs, molten lead from the roof poured out from a gargoyle's mouth and a water drain pipe before solidifying in the cold winter air of 14 November 1940 (following page).

Smoking ruins of St Michael's. (Photos Rob Orland and Gerry van Tonder)

(Photo Gerry van Tonder)

(Photo Gerry van Tonder)

As one of the guard descended a steep ladder down to the Cappers Room to fetch more water, the blast from a high-explosive bomb flung him from the ladder, smashing his head against the wall. His steel helmet, however, saved him from any serious injury.

At this time, another batch of incendiaries rained down, four striking the Girdlers' Chapel roof, but with supplies of water and sand running out, the guard's fire-fighting efforts were fruitless. Fires then broke out above the Children's Chapel.

A hologram-like image (depicted below) conjures up the grandeur of the main nave, with rows of chairs, flanked by tall columns, leading down to the reredos and the imposing arched stained-glass windows – now only a memory in history translated onto paper.

Filled with grief and realizing they could do no more, the four men gathered as many church ornaments as they could, before retiring to the south porch where they anxiously waited for the fire brigade.

When they arrived, however, after only a few minutes the flow of water through the hoses stopped. With 'consternation and horror', the church guard looked on as the fire engulfed the Children's and Lady chapels' roofs.

An hour later, the water supply had been restored but it was of low pressure. Torn between trying to save the iconic place of worship or saving lives elsewhere, the fire brigade was forced to withdraw.

Tarrying a little longer, the cathedral's provost then gathered the colours of the 7th Battalion, The Royal Warwickshire Regiment, that had been laid up in the sanctuary, the altar service book and books of epistles and gospels, and walked over to the police station in

A window in time – the grandeur of pre-Blitz St Michael's. (Photos Rob Orland and Gerry van Tonder)

The colours of the 7th Battalion, The Royal Warwickshire Regiment were saved from the inferno that destroyed the Cathedral. (Photos Rob Orland and Gerry van Tonder)

St Mary Street, where he left these items for safekeeping. They would be the last things to be taken from St Michael's as the fire consumed the building.

From 11 p.m. to 1.30 a.m., the provost looked on at the 'gradual and terrible destruction of the Cathedral'. As the roof collapsed, the stone pillars of the main nave and clerestory walls started falling over. Emotionally and physically exhausted, the provost later related how, in the 'seething mass of flame and piled-up blazing beams and timbers', he observed a flare of flame as the historic organ, once played by the eighteenth-century composer George Frideric Handel, burned.

Repair and restoration work demanded the skills of hundreds of local artisans:

COVENTRY NEEDS CARPENTERS
Unemployed carpenters, joiners, and other wood-workers residing in Coventry, who have not already registered at the Coventry Employment Exchange are asked to do so at once. Their services are urgently required for reconstruction work. If they are available for only a few days, their help will be of great value.

Cutting Tackle Needed
An urgent appeal is issued to all owners of acetylene cutting pipes and gauges to lend them for the purpose of cutting away girders and metal work in Coventry's damaged buildings and so expediting the work of demolishing and clearing away debris. This request concerns private owners as well as firms possessing such equipment. All tackle should be taken to Mr H. P. Jackson, Conduits Yard, Fleet Street, Coventry.

Asbestos and Timber Structures
The Corporation have made arrangements to erect, at reasonable cost, shop premises, to be constructed of asbestos and timber framing, and any person in the central areas, particularly those engaged in central trades, are invited to get in touch with the City Treasurer, without delay, expressing their wishes for or against opening on new sites.

In this way it is hoped to cater for the essential needs of the public in the way of clothing, drapery, tobacconists, chemists, dysalters [sic], boots and shoes, grocery, meat, butter, and other things.

The Midland Daily Telegraph, Friday, 22 November 1940)

Whilst the demise of St Michael's was entirely due to incendiary bombs, a high-explosive bomb detonated to the south-east of the building, leaving permanent scars in the stone walls from that fateful night (pictured below).

Back at Holy Trinity, a high-explosive bomb exploded next to the belfry. Clearing the rubble, Clitheroe and Thornton managed to extinguish a fire that was taking hold of the belfry's old oak timbers. No sooner had the two men returned to the vestry when a second bomb exploded outside on the path that the two of them had just walked on. Thankful to his Maker that it was only a 'little fellow' – most likely an SC50 – Clitheroe spoke modestly of the fact that 'it only made a hole twenty feet across, and perhaps ten or twelve feet deep'. He did concede, however, that it 'was enough to cause a crack in the great walls of the Archdeacon's Court'. Thornton reportedly exclaimed the mundane, 'My, but it's a funny life!'

(Photo Gerry van Tonder)

(Photo Gerry van Tonder)

(Photos Ministry of Information and Wikimedia)

By this time, fires were burning uncontrollably in all four cardinal directions of the city. As they awaited the dawn, Clitheroe wondered 'how all the dead would be buried'.

After the raid had passed, Clitheroe made his way in the dark to the vicarage on Radford Road and St Nicholas Street. He had to know if his family had survived the night. He described what he saw in the city centre as being one of 'indescribable havoc'. Rubble had replaced family homes. Particularly shocking was the twisted corrugated-iron remains of Anderson shelters that had taken direct hits. Clitheroe started realizing that the death toll from the night of carnage was going to be high.

The Highlands Nursing Home was a burned-out shell, and the Grey Lodge Hotel next to his home was a raging inferno. The vicarage had taken a hit just after midnight, but the percussion-type bomb only damaged the roof. St Nicholas Church in Radford had been levelled by a heavy-calibre bomb, killing the men of the fire guard and blinding Reverend John Lister, the church curate in charge of the guard.

At the Coventry and Warwickshire Hospital, exploding bombs severed the facility's electricity supply and blew out most of the windows in the buildings – it was reported that only 100 of the hospital's 1,600 windows were still intact. The expansive dressings stores were destroyed with their contents, and the medical and eye wards badly damaged. The laundry was demolished, while nursing staff quarters took direct hits. Water was running out and operations were being conducted in three theatres using emergency power. Remarkably, a driver and a volunteer nurse, killed in the hospital courtyard, were the hospital's only fatalities. Inside, it was a bitterly cold night for the patients, many cowering on the floor as bombs continued to explode. Hot drinks could not be made.

Coventry and Warwickshire Hospital main entrance, 1930s. (Photo Rob Orland)

Troops patrolled the city after heavy raids. (Photos Ministry of Information and Gerry van Tonder)

Along Broadgate, the scene was one of total chaos as fire tenders, firemen, hoses, cars, debris, fire and choking smoke clogged the once prosperous shopping and commercial hub of the city. Boots the Chemist had taken a direct hit, while Owen Owen, not for the first time since the start of the Blitz, was ablaze. All the while, bombs continued to rain down.

Astley's paint shop took a second hit, the burning paint adding to the heat and fumes. In the explosion, a water mains was hit, effectively severing Broadgate's lifeline. Like St Michael's, it would have to be left to burn.

At 6.15 a.m., Friday, 15 November, the all-clear sounded. Gas and water mains had been fractured in hundreds of places. The city's tram system would forever remain inoperable. Fires raged in front of Council House, but through the smoke, the site of a bomb explosion to the right of the entrance could be seen, while the walls of the building bore scores of shrapnel pockmarks, many untouched to this day (see the following page).

For Coventry's air defences, it had been an incredibly trying night, in which they had made no impact on the German bombers.

In April 1939, following the ominous resurgence of Germany's military power and Prime Minister Chamberlain's failed peace mission to Munich, the 95th (Birmingham) Heavy Anti-Aircraft Regiment, Royal Artillery, was formed as a home-defence precautionary measure. By early August, 293 Battery, one of four making up the regiment, had taken up station at B and L gun sites in Coventry.

After the outbreak of war, as part of a rationalization exercise, 293 Battery returned to Birmingham, their sites in Coventry taken up by outside batteries. Following his appointment

Cleaning up on the front of Council House. (Photos David McGrory and Gerry van Tonder)

Shrapnel scars at the entrance to Council House. (Photo Gerry van Tonder)

Cramped interior of the rudimentary Anderson shelter. (Photo Gerry van Tonder)

as ADC of Coventry on 16 September, the regiment's commanding officer, Lieutenant Colonel J. H. Lawrence OBE, MC, TD, DL, moved his headquarters to Rosehill, a large private country house on St Nicholas Street. At the same time, 204 Battery was deployed to site A at Longford.

At each site, there were four Ordnance QF 3.7in. guns, served by a concrete command post that held the various spotting and ranging instruments. A total of forty of these high-angle guns were operated on the 14th. On 12 November, a dozen Swedish-made 40mm Bofors light anti-aircraft guns arrived in Coventry to complement the heavy guns.

The citizens of Coventry had found shelter where they could: public street shelters, domestic Anderson shelters, cellars, or makeshift indoor Morrison 'shelters'.

Early in 1940, the government initiated a programme of providing communal street shelters in towns and cities deemed particularly vulnerable. Erected by private contractors under government supervision, the simple structures had thick brick walls with a reinforced-concrete roof. The walls, however, proved a major weakness, crumbling under heavy bombardment and causing the heavy roof to collapse and crush the occupants.

During the conflict, some three million Anderson shelters were built *in situ* across Britain. Named after the designer, Sir John Anderson, they were free to all households with an income of less than £250 per annum. For those who had to purchase the shelter, the price was £7. The structure could accommodate up to six people. The basic construction of the shelter comprised a curved roof and panelled walls, all of corrugated iron. This compartment was then covered with a metre-thick layer of soil, planted with turf to retain its integrity. Inside,

Morrison shelter for indoor use. (Photo Ministry of Information)

water often seeped in and they were always bitterly cold. The Anderson afforded greater protection from side blasts than the street shelters, but when they sustained a direct hit, the survival rate for the occupants tended to be nil.

Named for the Minister of Home Security, Herbert Morrison, the eponymous shelter was delivered in kit form free to those earning less than £350 a year. The shelter was made up of a prefabricated steel frame with a solid steel top, in much the same dimensions of an average kitchen table. The sides were covered in wire mesh. Whilst it was a known fact that it would not withstand a direct hit, the shelter, of which around 500,000 were manufactured, would provide good protection from falling masonry and timber.

(Ministry of Information)

Government, more out of moral support and caring, offered advice on how to prepare for a night in a shelter. Cold was the biggest cause of discomfort, but people were warned against the use of open fires for fear of carbon monoxide poisoning.

Luftwaffe operational maps found after the war clearly showed the sites of factory targets. For the staff of the emergency services and those doing their best to retaliate against the air attack, there could be little consideration for seeking a safe haven from the unremitting fall of incendiaries and bombs. The firemen fought a losing battle against scattered fires too numerous to attend to.

George Collier, Chief Fire Officer, of the Humber Works Fire Brigade, in spite of personal injury, was unrelenting in his efforts to control fires caused by incendiaries. His bravery, as laid out in his citation, earned Collier the George Medal:

Chief Officer Collier throughout showed great zeal and gallantry in directing the Works Fire.

Brigade when the city was subjected to a heavy air raid. At one time when endeavouring to prevent flames from spreading he climbed to the top of the building. The building collapsed, and although hurt by his fall, he carried on his duties. Later, he continued to put out incendiary bombs although on three occasions H.E. bombs actually exploded in the building in which he was working. He was injured in the back by debris from one of them, but although in considerable pain he continued to direct his Second and Third Officers. It was not until the end of the raid that he would permit himself to be taken to the Surgery and then on to the Hospital.

Alfred Herbert fire tender. (Photos Snowmanradio and Gerry van Tonder)

In previous raids Chief Officer Collier has also shown great fearlessness and zeal, and he and his Brigade have dealt with several fires with great efficiency.

The London Gazette, 13 December 1940

Around 30,000 incendiary devices saturated Coventry that night. Characteristically, upon striking the ground or a building, the bomb would ignite, but it was only after a brief while that a delayed detonation cap would cause an explosion that sprayed burning phosphorus in every direction. Many firefighters and ARP volunteers suffered serious burns from such unexpected explosions. The large engineering companies, such as Alfred Herbert and Daimler, had their own works' fire brigades, typically comprising tenders, fuel-driven water pumps and a team of trained firefighters. Their role in tackling widespread building fires was critical, especially when taking into account the large number of incendiaries that were used against the city.

Only Christ Church's spire survived the Blitz. (Photos Ministry of Information and Gerry van Tonder)

(Photos courtesy © Rolls Royce Heritage Trust, Derby and Gerry van Tonder)

On Broadgate, a furnace of heated air blew from the direction of St Michael's, further fanning the fires in Marks & Spencer and Woolworths opposite. At 8.10 p.m., voluntary firemen from the Rootes Works in Humber Park were despatched to Owen Owen on Broadgate, Coventry's only departmental store. The building, bombed before, was burning out of control when the team arrived, so they moved on to Hales Street instead, where there was a ready source of water from the River Sherbourne. Joining another group of firefighters, they tackled Warico Fireplaces, and Anslow's, a dealer in second-hand furniture. Debris damage to their fire hoses, multiple ruptured gas mains and the constant fall of incendiaries meant the firemen's efforts were hopeless.

Fire units at the Armstrong Siddeley and Alvis works were equally unsuccessful. At the former's works, the building at No. 4 Gate, on the corner of Parkside and Puma Way, was completely gutted. After clearing away all the debris, the brick shell was all that remained (depicted above).

To First World War veteran Campbell Joseph Kelly OBE, MC, MM, control officer of the Works Air Defence, bravery and disregard for personal safety appeared to be second nature. After attending to a fire at his own factory, Kelly led a team of twelve to assist with a large blaze in the

British Empire Medal.
(Photo The Saleroom)

city centre. After attending to a second fire, he was returning to his post when he stopped to assist with the recovery of the bodies of policemen trapped under a pile of debris, the result of a high-explosive bomb explosion. By 5 a.m., Kelly continued to give inspiring leadership to his spent team. Like all the other working parties, there was no cover as they concentrated on their tasks. Kelly was recognized for his work by being awarded the George Medal. His first officer, David Lloyd, was awarded the British Empire Medal.

As the night wore on, firemen from other centres joined their colleagues in the monumental task of saving the whole of Coventry from burning to the ground. Fifty-two came from Bristol, fifty from Leeds, and even London sent forty-eight. Individual pumps with attending crews arrived from Birmingham, nearby Kenilworth, Rugby, Nuneaton, Stratford-upon-Avon and Leamington.

At the 22-acre Alfred Herbert machine-tool works, seven members of the works' fire brigade were killed while battling a blaze. Four of them were still in their teens – Peter Robbins was only sixteen. Eddie Brown, brother to Dennis who was one of the seven firemen who perished, when hearing of what had happened, rushed on his bicycle to a first-aid clearing station established at the Stoney Stanford Swimming Baths, hoping to find that Dennis had survived. No sooner had he arrived when the public pool took a direct hit. The 16-year-old Eddie was also killed. Coventry's constabulary was not found wanting that night either. To them fell the equally hazardous duty of initiating and organizing the safe and orderly evacuation of unsafe properties or from the vicinity of unexploded bombs. Frequently, the latter were delayed-action bombs of indeterminate time to detonation.

(Photo Gerry van Tonder)

(Photos Ministry of Information and Wikimedia)

Special Constable Brandon, a fitter at Armstrong Siddeley Motors, started his volunteer shift at 11 p.m. that night. When a house was struck by a high-explosive bomb and completely demolished, the occupants became entombed. Moss led a rescue party in clearing an entry to the trapped victims under extremely dangerous conditions owing to collapsing debris and leaking gas. When conditions became critically dangerous, on his own he worked his way through a space he had cleared and was responsible for the saving of the three persons alive.

He then diverted his attention to adjoining premises in which people had also been buried. Moss again led the rescue. An extract from his George Cross citation best describes his actions during the rescue work:

The workers became exhausted after many hours of work but Moss laboured unceasingly and inspiringly throughout the complete night, again with falling beams and debris around him, and as a result of his superhuman efforts and utter disregard for personal injury one person was rescued alive and four other bodies recovered. During the whole of the time of the rescue, bombs were dropping around and it was known that there was a delayed action bomb in the doorway of a tavern only 20 yards away.

Notwithstanding the massive toll on civilian life and property inflicted on Coventry on the night of 14 November, Göring's ostensible arms-of-war factory targets were also hit in no small measure.

Since the turn of the twentieth century, the industrial city was home to several munitions factories. With motor vehicle, bicycle and aero-engine production key to the local – and indeed national – economy, Coventry, already an acknowledged pre-war centre of sophisticated machine tooling, could easily convert its industries to war production. Coventry Ordnance Works, already an accomplished maker of 4.5in. and 15in. howitzers, naval guns and ammunition, was a leading example of the city's war-effort capabilities. During the Second World War, the city of 238,000 people accounted for 25 per cent of Britain's aero-engine production.

In October 1940, the Armstrong Siddeley Works, manufacturers of luxury motor cars and radial aero-engines, took five hits. On 14 November, the Burlington Works, the body shop part of the complex, bound by Puma Road to the north and Quarryfield Lane to the east, alone took twelve hits, including a delayed-action bomb in the main works. One of the propeller test houses was damaged, as were some of the production test houses, the gas-turbine machine shop, and welding and chassis-erecting sections.

On the other side of Puma Road, and to the east of Parkside, this part of the works took fourteen hits. Housing the company's extensive machine shops, where seemingly endless rows of machine tools jammed the interiors, the central and lower shops each sustained three high-explosive bomb hits. In the central machine shop, these included two oil bombs and one with a delayed-action fuse. The two main gates on Parkside each took two hits right next to each other.

Tooling a naval gun at the Coventry Ordnance Works. (Photo Rob Orland)

The remains of Armstrong Siddeley's No. 66 workshop. (Photos courtesy © Rolls Royce Heritage Trust, Derby and Gerry van Tonder)

Structural bomb damage at an Armstrong Siddeley workshop. (Photo courtesy © Rolls Royce Heritage Trust, Derby)

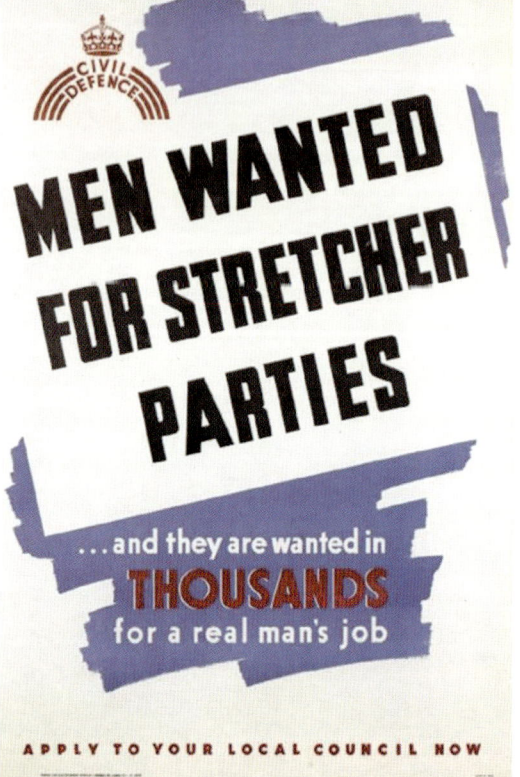

Above: Coventry and Warwickshire Hospital.
(Photo Rob Orland)

Left: (Photo IWM)

As a major wartime producer of armoured cars and aircraft components, the Daimler Works at Radford was a specific target for the Luftwaffe.

At the Coventry and Warwickshire Hospital, conditions were almost impossible. The building and the medical care infrastructure had suffered badly from the bombing. Medical staff, many of them volunteer stretcher-bearers and ambulance drivers who had already been at the normal jobs during the day, faced an overwhelming flood of casualties. At the hospital, scores of trestle tables had been set out earlier, but these proved wholly inadequate – the stream of victims with horrific shrapnel wounds and covered in dust gained momentum.

During the night, and in a short space of time, four high-explosive bombs fell on and around the St John Ambulance headquarters. Essential lines of communication were severed, forcing the brigade's ambulance operations to shift their base to the police station.

In recognition of their life-saving actions during the November raids, Miss Betty Quinn of the St John Ambulance Brigade, and Henry Norman Gregg, MB, ChB, MRCS, LRCP, Medical Officer of the Emergency Medical Service, were awarded the George Medal. Their respective citations read:

The George Medal.
(Photo MoD)

Miss Quinn was rendering voluntary service at an A.R.P. Post when a shower of incendiary bombs fell in the district. Without waiting for assistance she ran outside. At this time A.A. Batteries were putting up a heavy barrage and shrapnel was falling all round. Bombs began to fall and a man was injured by one. Miss Quinn assisted him to a public shelter. A report came in of an Anderson shelter receiving a direct hit and although bombs were still falling, Miss Quinn ran there and commenced digging in the crater with a spade. She remained there and assisted to dig out seven persons who had been trapped and then attended to their injuries. She stayed until all had been removed by ambulance although shells were bursting overhead the whole of the time. She then returned to the Post and carried on with her duties assisting distressed people there.

The London Gazette, 13 December 1940

When the City of Coventry was heavily bombed by enemy aircraft Dr. Gregg showed a high degree of courage and resource which contributed to the saving of a number of lives. While fires were raging and bombs falling, he coolly continued to go, partly on foot and partly by bicycle, from one incident to another administering morphia to those trapped in the wreckage, and applying first aid under conditions of extreme difficulty, with complete disregard for the intense bombardment and for the very real personal danger entailed.

The London Gazette, 14 January 1941

(Photo Rob Orland)

Daylight on 15 November revealed an horrific, smoke-filled, grey landscape, such as at Martin's Bank (pictured above) and Broadgate, the Union Flag defiant. It was reminiscent, to some, of the Western Front in the First World War. Many remained in ice-cold shelters, too scared to leave the relative safety. There was no gas or electricity supply, telephones were out, and water scarce. The fate of relatives and friends was an unknown. The dark tempest of the night, however, was over. Brittle nerves, raw emotions and aching bodies discovered that being alive was, when all was said and done, their good fortune. Life continued and the new day had to be faced.

Above: Pre-Blitz Broadgate a hive of activity of pedestrians, cyclists, trucks and buses. (Photos David McGrory and Gerry van Tonder)

Right: (Photo Wikimedia)

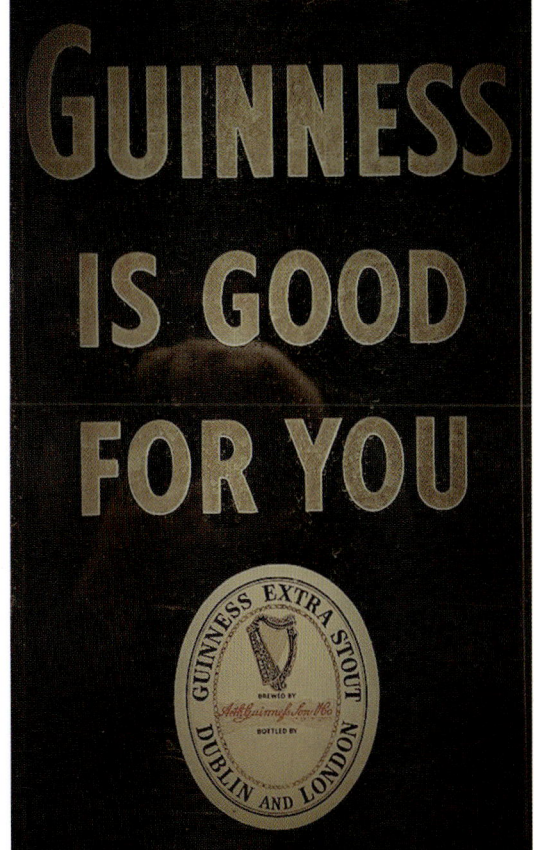

The tranquil green park setting of the mass graves. (Photos David McGrory and Gerry van Tonder)

The devastation was mind-numbing. Familiar life-long landmarks were gone. Just a few months ago, Broadgate was bustling with activity: trams, lorries, cyclists, and shoppers off to Owen Owen. Deep craters made many roads impassable. Fallen house walls compromised domestic privacy, but these residents still had a semblance of a dwelling place. For many others there was nothing. Almost everything the people of Coventry saw as they left their places of safety evoked despair. The essentials of life had to be met – food, shelter, warmth. Anguish would have defied description.

A few days after the moonlight raid, on the front page of the *Telegraph*, the brewers of Guinness extolled the physical- and mental-uplifting virtues of their alcoholic beverage: 'Guinness is Good for You'. Elaborating, 'It's good for strength when you're tired. It's good for nerves that are strained and "on edge". It's good to help you sleep at night'. The defiance and fortitude enshrined in the promise of a return to normality was very evident (previous page).

16–30 NOVEMBER

On Wednesday, 20 November, in an inter-denominational service led by the Bishop of Coventry, Dr Mervyn Haigh, 172 victims of the raid almost a week before, were laid to rest in the city's London Road Cemetery (pictured above). Deep trenches had been dug, into which the plain wooden coffins were stacked three deep. Addressing the 1,000-strong congregation, the bishop said that 'the eyes of millions of people were upon Coventry at the present time.' He strongly encouraged Coventry's citizens to lay down an oath before God 'to be better friends and neighbours in the future, because we have suffered this together and have stood here today.' The following Saturday there was a second burial service, in which another

250 bombing victims were interred in mass graves. In many cases, the 'remains' of those interred amounted to little more than body parts.

By the 25th, demolition work continued to recover bodies still missing from the bombing of the 14th, but city authorities believed that the number was 'not considerable'. The greatest number of fatalities in one spot was thirty-five, recovered from a collapsed city building.

A temporary mortuary had been established in an empty building at the gasworks where, the cold winter ensuring a chilled environment, bodies were stored pending mass burials. As bodies arrived and were placed on racks inside the building, administrative processing began with identification, where possible, followed by the issuing of death certificates. In many cases, clothing was the only way in which badly mutilated bodies could be identified. By the Monday, 380 bodies had been received at the mortuary. Thirty-eight bomb sites had still to be cleared, which would yield further fatalities. A constant stream of people thronged around one of the town house's side walls where Council was posting the latest casualty figures. Uncertainty about the fate of missing relatives and friends fuelled rumours of the authorities covering up the truth about the number of dead. A statement published by the *Telegraph* refuted the rumours. The appearance of armed troops throughout much of the city centre ensured that law and order were maintained. In addition to a battalion-strength of infantry, the military presence included elements of the Royal Engineers and Pioneer Corps. The War Office, however, objected to the use of military resources to help bring Coventry's industries back to levels approximating pre-war production. Western Command required their men for training and deployment to various theatres of war.

Council House today, a survivor of the Blitz. (Photo Gerry van Tonder)

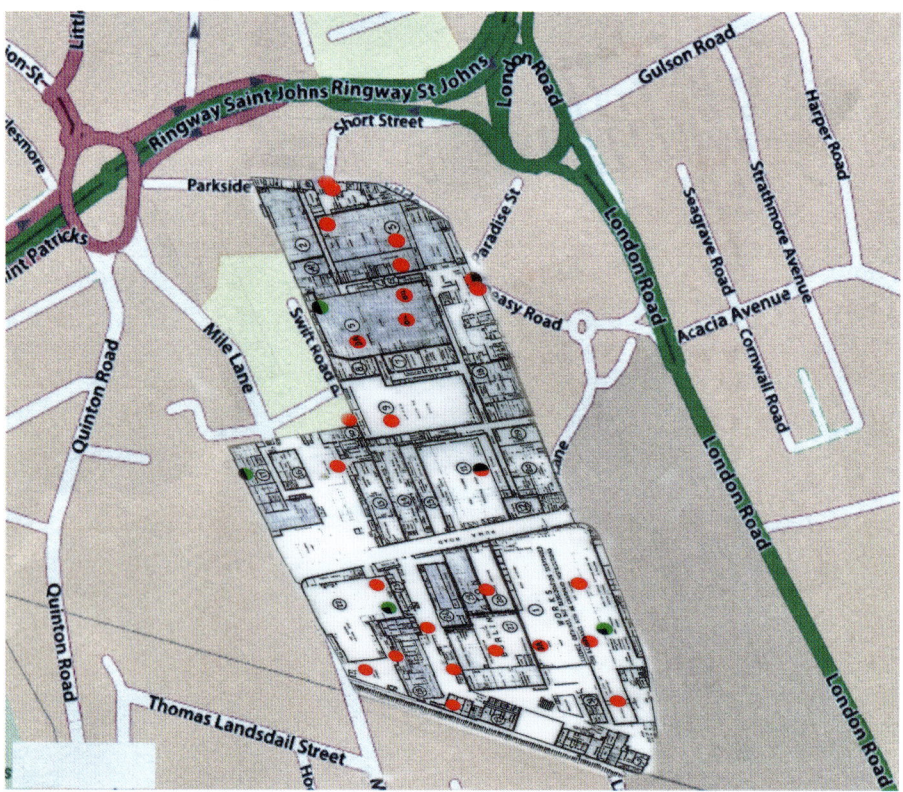

Above: The sprawling Armstrong Siddeley Works where it was once situated just south of what is today the St Johns Ringway. *Below*: A contemporary plan of the works showing damage sustained in 1940 raids'. (Image courtesy © Rolls Royce Heritage Trust, Derby)

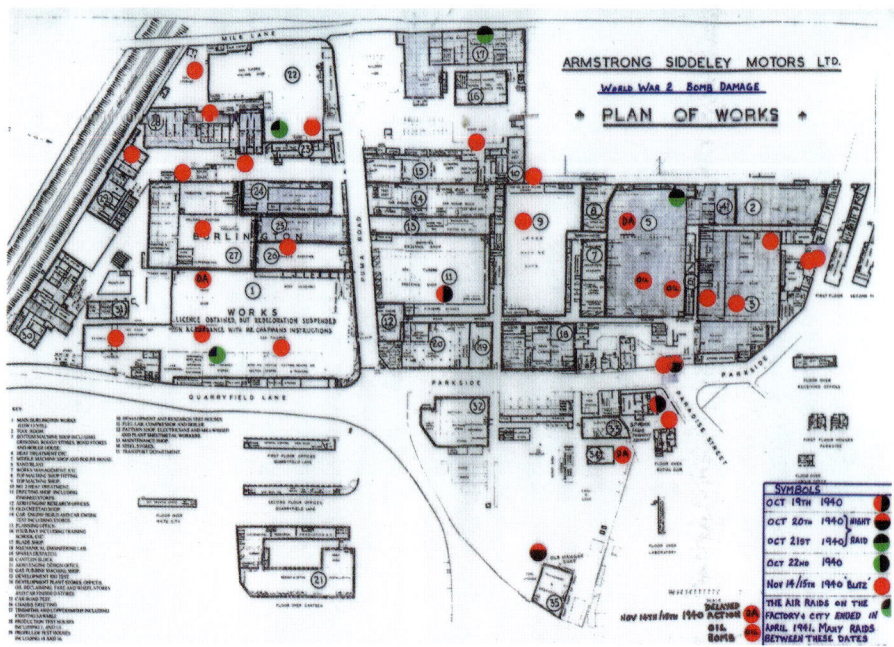

Minister of Home Security, Herbert Morrison, insisted that the restoration of Coventry's war effort capabilities was an imperative, but that this could only be achieved with the assistance of the army in expediting emergency repairs, thereby releasing scarce skilled civilian labour to return to their respective factories.

Feeding the stricken city had become an immediate priority, and mobile canteens and military kitchens soon started to appear. Much of the food recovered from the debris, especially in tins, had spoiled and therefore not fit for consumption. Milk and bread vendors from neighbouring centres set up temporary roadside stalls (such as pictured below), bringing much-needed relief. Wartime rationing was suspended and thirty tons of canned meat rushed to the city.

Supplies of potable water had been virtually severed, compounded by the fact that several of the city's pumping stations had also been badly damaged in the raid. Mile upon mile of piping was laid and water became available from standpipes. The sewerage system was not functioning, so the authorities instructed people to dig holes in their gardens to use as toilets.

More than 300 gas mains throughout the city had been holed, while the gasworks itself was severely damaged. One of the gas receptacles was destroyed. Although some of the electricity distribution substations sustained varying degrees of damage, the main transmission cables feeding Coventry remained intact.

Amidst the stench of death, mountains of debris and prevailing danger from unexploded bombs, factory workers were paid nominal rates to assist with the daunting task of trying to re-establish a semblance of order from the chaos. At the St John Ambulance station, the fins

(Photos David McGrory and Gerry van Tonder)

Extensive damage at Armstrong Siddeley. (Photo courtesy © Rolls Royce Heritage Trust, Derby)

of an 800lb unexploded bomb stuck out ominously from the ground. At Humber Hillman Motors to the south-east of the city centre, four men were killed when a delayed-action bomb exploded more than two days after it had been dropped.

Largely unnoticed by the general population, distracted by the King's morale-boosting visit, an inspector from the Ministry of Home Security was also in Coventry the Saturday after the raid. It was his finding that more than 30 per cent of Coventry's factories had either been completed destroyed or sufficiently damaged to disable production for several months. A similar number would only be out of production for a number of weeks, while other works miraculously escaped the bombing unscathed.

Jenkyn Shanklyn, a member of the Coventry Works Rescue Squad, displayed amazing physical endurance in the performance of his duties, as reflected in his citation for the Medal of the Civil Division of the Most Excellent Order of the British Empire, for meritorious service (BEM):

When Coventry experienced a very heavy enemy air attack Shanklyn's party was sent to where a large bomb had exploded and caused heavy devastation to private dwelling houses.

Shanklyn was the outstanding figure of the Rescue Party. He dug his way through the debris of two houses near the big bomb crater; and after an arduous task found

Right and below: Devastation to roofs at Armstrong Siddeley. (Photos courtesy © Rolls Royce Heritage Trust, Derby)

two bodies, which he dragged out and carried to ambulances. He searched further, removing bricks from the stairway, and rescued a female alive. She was conveyed to hospital in an ambulance.

Shanklyn continued his work in other parts of the town and throughout showed no regard for his own well-being or safety.

The London Gazette, 4 February 1941

[In the week following the raid, he recovered eighteen mangled corpses at Barracks Square and a further twenty-two badly burned bodies from the ruins of a hotel in Jordan Well.]

On the morning of Monday, the 18th, a multi-services meeting was held at Council House, one of few still usable, attended by officials from the various Corporation departments, staff from the Ministry of Health and representatives from the military stationed in the city. It was reported that while the restoration of gas supplies was ongoing, electricity and water were slowly being reconnected.

The meeting heard that there were very few houses in the city which had not been affected, but that residents were carrying out 'first-aid' repairs to their damaged homes. Scrap wood, cardboard and roof felt were being used to block out the cold weather.

The mayor had visited nearby Leamington to speak to homeless Coventry evacuees who had been given temporary housing in the town. In all, there were twenty-one such emergency facilities in operation to see to the welfare of those without shelter. In addition, local associations and societies such as the WVS, the Salvation Army and the YMCA, assisted with the establishment of a dozen relief stations strategically situated throughout the city to provide food and clothing. A further seventeen centres provided meals only, while the army was helping with field kitchens and mobile canteens. Food salvaged, such as bread from burned-out bakeries, was being offered for sale by street vendors.

During the meeting, the city water engineer, Mr E. J. Pugh, reported on 'wholesale' damage to the city's mains. Accordingly, he encouraged townspeople to conserve water at all times, and to undertake basic repairs to leaking pipes and taps themselves. In those areas which had been heavily bombed, a company from the Royal Engineers was assisting to lay temporary pipes, especially to those areas where there was no water at all. The city was warned to boil all drinking water.

The Corporation gas engineer reported on the 'unceasing efforts' of his department to restore supply. Until that happened, consumers would be instructed to shut the gas taps leading in to their meters.

In the absence of supplies of gas and water, since 14 November the Post Office Decontamination Centre on Cow Lane had been providing all-comers with free hot showers, in what was described as 'first-rate conditions'. The well-equipped station did its own laundry, thereby further augmenting what was on offer. A strict gender regime had been implemented, in which women used the amenities from 9 a.m. to 1 p.m., and the men from 2 to 5 p.m. Supervisor and anti-gas instructor Mr H. S. Somerfield boasted that no one was being turned away, which included use of the sanitary and water facilities under his control.

The civil defence section of the city's police force had been bombed out of their old premises and were now in temporary accommodation, but with only one telephone line. The police also reported that six individuals had been arrested at the peak of the raid on the Thursday: four for looting and two for breaking into shops.

Accurate casualty figures were yet to be collated, compounded by the difficulties being experienced by rescue teams to either rescue survivors to recover bodies from mountains of building rubble. It was feared that the initial estimate of fatalities may have been underestimated, and that numbers would include children.

That afternoon, the Ministry of Food's Midland Division invited the city's wholesalers to attend a meeting at the Coventry Food Office on Warwick Row, to make arrangements for the equitable distribution of food throughout the city. The wholesalers were informed that there were already sufficient supplies of food in the city, and that more was ready for shipment when required.

Emulating the example of London, Coventry's Director of Education, who also assumed the role of chief evacuation officer during the Blitz, made a public appeal for all school-going children, who had not yet done so, to be registered at his offices as soon as possible. The exercise covered the whole urban and peri-urban catchment, regardless of type of school – government or private. Teaching staff were also told to report to their respective schools to await further instructions.

December 1940

Sunday worship on the 1st provided further evidence of Coventry's desire to return to as normal a life as possible in extremely adverse conditions. Two city hotels made sections of their premises available for the congregations of St Francis of Assisi and St Nicholas churches to meet for services.

The Pilot Hotel on Catesby Road became the temporary venue for the Reverend J. P. Herbert of St Francis to minister to his flock. On the night of 14 November, the priest had been making cocoa for the occupants of a public shelter when a bomb exploded only 20yd from where he had been standing. The bomb wrecked his church while the blast flung him to the outside. He was unhurt. Herbert returned after the all-clear was sounded to recover vestments, ornaments and the altar top from the rubble. These he arranged in the hotel's assembly room, thereby creating a more spiritual ambiance. The hotel's piano was used to accompany the singing of hymns. The damaged church, which had only been built in 1939 to serve the new Radford Aerodrome and Hill Farm estates to meet an increased demand by the city's expanding car industry, re-opened on 13 March 1944. The present building was consecrated in January 1959 and the old church converted into a hall.

For the vicar of St Nicholas Church, also in Radford, things had been very different. Four young men, some of whom formed the church's fire guard, perished in the bombing, while the junior curate, Reverend J. F. Lister sustained serious injuries. At the Grapes public house, the vicar had to make do with a trestle table for an altar. Permission was also given for other equipment in the pub belonging to the local lodge of the Order of Druids to be used. The old St Nicholas – designed by George Taylor of Coventry as a chapel of ease to Holy Trinity Church and which was consecrated in September 1874 – was destroyed on 14 November. The new church, designed by the architect Richard Twentyman, was completed in 1957. In 1992, it was declared a listed building.

On Tuesday, 3 December, the full City Council met for the first time since the raid of 14 November. Chairman of the Housing Committee, Alderman Weston, reported that 4,200 of

St Francis of Assisi, Radford, Coventry, built 1958. (Photo Niki Walton)

St Nicholas, destroyed in the bombing raid in 14 November 1940. (Photo Rob Orland)

The new St Nicholas, opened in 1957. (Photo Robin Stott)

the Corporation's 5,800 houses had been damaged and 100 'totally demolished'. The rate of repair, conducted by a team of 1,400 building operatives, was 500 a day. The housing department had undertaken the enormous task of removing and storing furniture for safekeeping.

Council would also confirm the decisions made by the General Works Committee for the erection of temporary retail shops in council-owned vacant land on Corporation Street. City Architect Donald Gibson had been in the process of drawing up a standard design for the temporary structures, and was almost ready for the next stage of inviting tenancy applications. Only those individuals whose business outlets had been destroyed or declared unfit for purpose as a result of enemy action would be considered. Other Corporation premises not affected by the bombings would also be considered for letting out to retailers. By this time, thirty-five applications had been received.

The municipal cafeteria on Well Street was undergoing urgent repair to accommodate re-equipping. The head of Coventry's WVS, Councillor Pearl Hyde, informed the meeting that her organization was now operating seventy fully staffed canteens, providing 20,000 people with free food every day.

Christmas 1940 brought little cheer. There was a desperate shortage of skilled artisans – bricklayers, plasterers, plumbers, carpenters – to repair and rebuild domestic properties. More than 14,000 homes needed repair work done to make them safe for re-occupation. Inevitably, the vagaries of wartime bureaucracy slowed down the whole reconstruction process, with the Office of Works, the Board of Trade, local health authorities, council, the Ministry of Food and the Ministry of Supply all requiring procedures demanded by laid-down protocol and regulations.

Mobile canteens were integral to the immediate recovery process. (Photo Ministry of Information)

Mrs Pearl Marguerite Hyde, County Borough Organizer, for the Coventry WVS was appointed an additional Member of the Civil Division of the Most Excellent Order of the British Empire (MBE), for her courageous voluntary services during bombing raids. Her citation reads:

> Throughout the many enemy air raids on Coventry Mrs Hyde has shown conspicuous bravery in shepherding people to public shelters, visiting shelters during actual raids and encouraging the occupants by her unselfish devotion to duty in ministering to their wants.
>
> Mrs Hyde has assisted in the feeding of homeless people, showing disregard of danger in organising refreshments for the homeless and Civil-Defence Workers, and going herself when road conditions were perilous from falling masonry and debris, and from the presence of unexploded bombs.
>
> She continued this work for several days, but with little rest.
>
> *The London Gazette*, 4 February 1941

In an advert in the *Telegraph*, Trinity Street retailer, John Barry, in a show of resilience and defiance, proclaimed:

Member of the Order of the British Empire. (Photo MoD)

WE CARRY ON ... with the same fervour, the same striving to produce garments of exclusive and distinctive designs that drew your admiration before the 'Blitz.'

TO-DAY we feature warm coats in the new Camopile, the new Alpaca materials that are to-day's essential fashion; our woollen dresses have never been smarter.

CARRY ON

5

APRIL 1941

St Michael's Cathedral Memorial. (Photo Gerry van Tonder)

'Industry is on its toes, but it depends on the insistent and persistent effort of every individual to give of the very best in the national effort, and work as though victory relies on him or her personally. We shall win through all right, but the time factor is governed by the personal efforts of everyone.'

Cllr G. E. Roberts, president of the Coventry Chamber of Commerce
in his New Year appeal

JANUARY 1941

Early in January, and arising out of the very recent 'great-fire raid' on London, Minister of Home Security Herbert Morrison announced that the Fire Watchers' Order of September 1940 would be amended to make local fire-watching schemes compulsory throughout Britain. Drawing attention to the Coventry experience, especially during the 14 November raid,

St Michael's spire. (Photo Gerry van Tonder)

Morrison made the accusation that many parts of the country remained apathetic towards committing themselves to looking after their own properties. The capital's population came under specific criticism for being convinced that the widespread damage caused by fire-bombs was the fault of both local and central government for not providing adequate and sufficient fire-fighting squads in all the city's major buildings.

The lessons learned from Coventry and other provincial towns and cities, where individual teams of fire guards looked after their own premises and houses, had not been heeded in other places such as London. Political commentators in the capital lauded Coventry's unilateral efforts to safeguard their own city, saying that, albeit small consolation, good had come out of their misery at the hands of the Luftwaffe.

Industrial, commercial and spiritual leaders of the stricken city addressed the advent of 1941 with encouragement and hope for a better future. Following a stirring message in the ruins of St Michael's Cathedral on Christmas day, Coventry provost, the Very Reverend R. T. Howard, addressed the city's workers, saying, 'We are sweating and suffering not merely for victory and the peace afterwards, but because we long to make a better England, a better world – let's not be afraid of the word – a Christian England.'

Reverend Leslie Cooke spoke of disaster as a 'glorious opportunity and a fellowship of suffering,' arising out of which thoughts of 'a new and lovelier city, better planned and better housed, arising from the ruins of the old. The modern Coventry, which in many ways had the charms and failings of adolescence has, through its sorrows, stepped into maturity.'

8 JANUARY 1941

On the afternoon of 8 January, the Luftwaffe reminded Coventry that it had not been forgotten. A low-flying daylight raider dropped three heavy-calibre, high-explosive bombs over a residential area. Although several houses were damaged, there were no reported casualties. One bomb fell on a sports ground, another on a football pitch and a third on a vegetable garden 10ft from the house. In Berlin, the German Press Association claimed that, in spite of barrage balloons and anti-aircraft fire from the city's defences, their bomber scored two direct hits on a Coventry factory.

13 JANUARY 1941

At this time, the president of the Board of Education toured Coventry to assess for himself the massive disruption that the bombing raids had caused to schooling. In Cheylesmore, school facilities no longer existed. Not a single school was left between Wheatley Street and Willenhall. Efforts to transport school pupils long distances to external schools had failed miserably. Permission had to be sought from the central education authorities for the erection of a temporary building.

FEBRUARY 1941

Local authorities revealed that City Architect Donald Gibson's redevelopment plan for a new Coventry had been accepted on the basis that it would be completed in a span of five years. Refusing to be drawn on cost, Gibson pointed out that the damage to buildings in the city centre's retail district was so great that reconstruction could commence as soon as the war ended – by then the plans would be complete and ready for immediate implementation.

Questioned about the main thoroughfare into the centre, Gibson stated that Hertford Street would continue as the principal arterial route until such time as the development of the city centre was complete. He envisaged that a new street would follow the course of Greyfriars Lane before changing direction to head for the train station. The two bank buildings would also go to accommodate the new road. He believed that it would be far more advantageous to relocate the ancient Ford's Hospital, rather than just rebuilding it on the same spot. All such buildings constituted an important part of the city's heritage, so a specially reserved site for all these treasures would be set aside. Smithford Street would cease to exist, thereby finally ridding the city of traffic congestion.

Time, however, would show that Gibson did not get it all his way. It would be a difficult journey. Accusations of feet-dragging and incompetence were already starting to surface, as did the rumour of a rebuilding cost of £40 million. Gibson's plans were being criticized in some quarters as being too ambitious.

Since the big raid the previous November, there had been the occasional fleeting daylight raid by lone bombers, dropping few bombs and machine-gunning random ground targets. Arguably, Coventry's citizens could not be blamed for believing that their baptism of fire had not ended.

MARCH 1941

In yet another irony in the life of the battered Coventry, rubble had a meaningful value as opposed to use as landfill. *The Midland Daily Telegraph* of 17 March, reported that bricks, usually unavailable to most, could be had for £2 a thousand after being sorted out from the bomb rubble. Broken bricks and unsalvageable rubble were being used in road construction, while timber and bricks were useful for patching up bomb damage to residential properties.

Rubble was fetching 10s for 2 tons and broken beams and splintered timber had a ready market as firewood at 30s for a 2-ton lorry load.

In the early days of clearing rubble, looters tapped into the lucrative metals black market. Earlier in the month, a room full of pilfered lead was found in an abandoned building. Under the direction of the Controller of Metal Salvage, however, such theft was quickly eradicated. Strict controls were introduced to ensure that all metal salvaged went towards the all-important war effort. Non-ferrous metals were sorted and despatched to refineries. The baser metals were sent to steel works – copper was attracting £52 a ton and lead £18. More than 2,000 tons of metal was salvaged during March.

During the night of 23/24 March, the RAF conducted its 38th raid of the war on Berlin.

At the end of the month, Coventry Bishop Dr Mervyn Haigh announced that contributions to the fund for the rebuilding of the cathedral were being loaned to government for the war effort.

APRIL 1941

At the beginning of the new month, London boasted eleven successive 'bomb-free' nights. Raids had been scattered, although the north-east coast had received concentrated attention.

On the 2nd, however, Hitler's litany of aerial slaughter claimed another victim in Coventry. While out playing on his tricycle, the hapless 3-year-old Raymond Jones drowned when he plunged into a large bomb crater filled with water. The waste land had previously been fenced off, but the blast of the bomb had ripped a hole in the barrier.

In Coventry, on Saturday the 5th, the cathedral was re-opened to the public for the first time since its destruction in November. An iron safe, recovered from the ruins, was put on display to encourage visitors to contribute to the cathedral's rebuilding fund. A team of church staff, led by cathedral mason Jock Forbes, who incidentally had been on fire-watch that night, had toiled over the last four and a half months to clear a large section of the nave of rubble. Forbes had constructed a new altar, using material from the debris, on the site where the original altar had been destroyed.

A souvenir booklet was produced that, with the use of photographs and ancient drawings, tracked the history of St Michael's, went on sale to also contribute to the reconstruction fund. Historical watersheds mentioned in the cathedral's life dated back to 1043, when Earl Leofric and Lady Godiva established a Benedictine monastery and erected a Norman priory in the area of Priory Row, through to the visit of George VI two days after the cathedral met its fate.

Former sub-Dean of Coventry, Bishop Meterman, was inspired to write this verse in the autograph book of a young girl from the congregation in Leamington:

St. Michael's Spire
In other years, when you look back
Along life's unforgotten track
And see our great St. Michael's spire
Soar upward like a tongue of fire,
Will it be pleasant to recall
How golden shafts of sunlight fall
Across the nave from windows decked
By some forgotten architect?
And will it help you to be true

Holy Trinity and the spire of St Michael's. (Photo Gerry van Tonder)

To all the best you meant to do
If sometimes, seeing far away
St. Michael's spire, on some clear day,
You say 'As over field and hill
St. Michael's spire points skyward still,
So let my heart, where'er I roam
Each up each day to Heaven its home'?
Quoted in *The Midland Daily Telegraph*, Saturday, 5 April 1941

HOLY WEEK APRIL 1941

In ecclesiastical terms, the days on which Easter is celebrated each year, are determined by the so-called Paschal full moon. In 1941, Good Friday fell on 11 April, so the horrors of aerial bombardments revisited on Coventry that week became known as the Holy Week or Easter raids.

8–9 APRIL 1941

On the night of Tuesday, 8 April, the Reverend Clitheroe was, as was his routine, on the roof of his beloved Holy Trinity Church. Having grown accustomed to quieter nights, he was alone while Kenneth Thornton and Basil White, members of the guard that night, caught up on much-needed sleep. Shortly after 9 p.m., the city's air-raid sirens started to sound. Whilst alert, Clitheroe knew that there had been more than fifty such 'cautionary' alarms since November – this was likely yet another. However, the approaching thuds of detonating incendiary bombs brought home the reality that another night raid had commenced.

Over the next almost seven hours, 230 German bombers crossed the night sky over Coventry, dropping 350 tons of high-explosive bombs and 25,000 incendiaries. The raid left 281 dead.

The following day, the *The Midland Daily Telegraph* banner headline shouted, 'Coventry Again Ravaged by Nazi Vandals'. An initial 'short and sharp' attack, in which thousands of incendiaries were dropped, was followed by a 'longer raid of considerable intensity'.

Particularly hard hit was the Coventry and Warwickshire Hospital, sustaining no fewer than ten direct hits. Two doctors, seven nurses, three stretcher-bearers and twenty-one patients perished. In the hospital's entrance hall, a number of off-duty nurses were having a rest when a massive explosion brought down the two floors above them. A bomb also crashed into an operating theatre, but fortunately the room had been cleared only moments earlier. Two members of staff and a patient were killed when the X-ray department took a direct hit. The switchboard operator that night had just taken the decision to leave his post as the raid had knocked out the hospital's telephone communications, when a bomb exploded where he had been sitting only moments before. Having narrowly escaped certain death, the man dashed back to the scene, where he rescued a patient whose face was the only part of his body showing in the debris. Underneath the patient he was shocked to find a young nurse, whom he also managed to extract. Only a few scratches gave any indication of her terrifying ordeal.

Tragically, the greatest number of casualties took place at 7 a.m. after the all-clear had sounded, when a delayed-action bomb exploded. Not a single window in the badly damaged hospital building remained intact. There was no heat and no water. Incoming casualties had to be transported out of Coventry.

Coventry and Warwickshire Hospital – all the windows shattered. (Photo David McGrory)

The situation in the battered Coventry and Warwickshire Hospital had become extremely hazardous. The duties of medical staff suddenly extended to include those of firefighter, rescuer and counsellor. Sidney Cecil Hill, House Governor and Secretary, Miss Joyce Elizabeth Burton, Matron, and Miss Emma Horne, Nursing Sister, were deservedly awarded the George Medal for their unsolicited courage and devotion to their patients. This is very evident in their citations:

During an enemy air attack the hospital was heavily damaged by direct hits from H.E. bombs.

Mr Hill worked all night during and after the raid. He led parties to put out fires and to extricate patients from the ruined wards. After the explosion of a time bomb which wrecked part of the basement, he led a party down one of the tunnels, and at great risk, rescued a number of patients. His unselfish devotion to duty and his courage were an inspiration to others and he was instrumental in the saving of many lives.

Miss Burton went round the wards throughout the raid regardless of personal danger, cheering the patients and encouraging her nursing staff. Whenever a ward was hit she was quickly on the scene, directing and helping with the rescue work. By her courage and example she was largely responsible for the high morale of the patients and nursing staff.

Miss Burton showed great devotion to duty in extremely dangerous conditions.

Sister Horne was on duty on the second floor, when a direct hit carried away the end of a ward. She reassured the patients and spared no efforts to evacuate them to the basement. Two other wards then received direct hits and Sister Horne went to these wards and, regardless of personal danger, she helped to pull patients from the wreckage and remove them to safety. Later she managed to release a junior nurse who was trapped under debris and stayed with her in conditions of great danger until further help came. Afterwards, for some hours Sister Horne worked unceasingly in the most difficult conditions to help evacuate the patients. By her efforts during the night many lives were saved.

The London Gazette, / July 1941

Several firemen died in the raid, including three who were killed instantly when their AFS post canteen took a direct hit. The widow of a volunteer fireman killed in the November raid also lost her life.

At St Mary's Police Station, a high-explosive bomb detonated in the entrance of the building, killing Special Constabulary Commander Arthur Frederick Matts MBE, Special Constable H. J. Pemberton of the Mobile Section and Special Constable Frank Kimberley. Eight other regular and volunteer members of the forces were injured when a large section of the station building collapsed. PC Shirley, who had been on duty at the entrance, was thrown across the street by the explosion. Matts had only been awarded the MBE in March for 'leadership, initiative and devotion to duty'.

Adjacent to the burned-out shell of St Michael's Cathedral on Bayley Lane, the historic St Mary's Guildhall took several incendiaries, damaging the lead roof and setting fire to the timber structures underneath. According to the *Telegraph*, firemen were still fighting the fire the next day.

(Ministry of Health)

On Warwick Road, the King Henry VIII School, founded in 1545, was badly damaged. The school, however, remained open, offering the full curriculum to its 820 pupils.

In addition to the railway station, the Armstrong Siddeley, Courtaulds and Daimler works took hits.

In a first, RAF fighters arrived, accounting for six of the bombers. One aircraft crashed in the county, while others only reached Leicestershire and Hertfordshire before crashing. In its Wednesday, 9 April edition, the *The Midland Daily Telegraph* carried an account related by a Hurricane pilot who had dealt with two Heinkel He 111s. The airman takes up his story after he had fired into the fuselage of a bomber:

> After the explosion, the flames ripped along the fuselage as the Heinkel pilot twisted and turned in an attempt to evade a second attack. He managed to get into the shelter of a cloud, but I followed, and when I broke through on the other side, the machine was ablaze and incendiaries and bombs kept on exploding as the flames reached them. The machine eventually hit the ground and exploded in a mass of flames.
>
> I climbed again and almost at once picked up the second Heinkel. This one gave me a bit of a fight, for bullets from the rear gunner hit my wing. Oil poured from it and came back and covered my windscreen. I had to break away while I cleaned the windscreen with my glove before I could see to deliver any more attacks. After my next burst of fire both motors were burning and there were flames inside the fuselage.

Clearing the tracks and platform at the railway station. (Photos Snowmanradio and Rob Orland)

Hawker Hurricanes. (Photo RAF)

A Coventry bus totally destroyed during a bombing raid. (Photos Ministry of Information and Gerry van Tonder)

From his vantage point on the roof of Holy Trinity Church, Reverend Clitheroe could see incendiary fires 'in all directions'. In a deafening din, anti-aircraft guns responded as bombs fell among the buildings. In between extinguishing the odd incendiary that landed on his church's roof, Clitheroe and his guard made coffee over on a primus stove. Starting to feel that the raid was of 'heavier stuff' than that of November, shrapnel hitting the church roof and denting the lead made him comment wryly that 'it was unhealthy up there!'

At around midnight, there was a tangible lull in the raid. Describing how, when the moonlit night had become still, with not a murmur from guns or aircraft, Clitheroe dashed home to check on his family. Fires raged everywhere, including in the direction of his house. As he approached the area, however, he discovered that King Henry VIII Grammar School was ablaze. In spite of the efforts of the headmaster and a guard of senior pupils, it was Clitheroe's assessment that 'this fine school was being burned out'.

Apart from a bomb that had exploded next door, shattering windows in his house, Clitheroe was relieved to find his family safe. Nearby, however, he had seen 'many dead' by a shelter that appeared to have taken a direct hit. A short while later, the bombing recommenced, and the city 'again suffered heavily with many killed and injured'.

In *The London Gazette* of 5 August 1941, Corporal John Duggan of a Coventry first-aid party, and Norman Nowell, member of a rescue party in the city, were rewarded with the George Medal and the British Empire Medal respectively, for their selfless actions during air raids. Their citations read:

> During an enemy air attack Duggan took his squad to a building which had received a direct hit. It was a mass of ruins and was blazing furiously. While bombs were exploding all around, Duggan worked desperately under the most hazardous conditions in an attempt to reach trapped persons. From this incident he went to another where, at great personal risk, he rescued several seriously wounded persons. He constantly exposed himself to danger in order to reach casualties and his courage was a source of inspiration to the men of his squad.
>
> Nowell showed great gallantry and lack of thought for his own safety in tunnelling under fallen debris consisting of an upper floor and the greater part of a roof, to release one person trapped by the ankles; he also tunnelled further to get at a person trapped under the stairs who could not be released from above until bricks and debris holding him from the waist downwards had been cleared. This could only be done by handing back from underneath. The whole operation took nearly two hours. Gas was escaping in the building, but Nowell would not have a relief owing to risk of debris falling whilst changing over. All this was done whilst Nowell was laying full length on the floor. He was affected by the gas but recovered later.

Berlin again claimed that factories of 'military importance' had been heavily bombed in Coventry. At a meeting in Council House the next day, called by Regional Commissioner Lord Dudley, seconded government officials and civic heads met around the table to review and speed up the city's reconstruction. Chairman of the Coventry Industrial Coordination Committee, William Rootes, confirmed that Coventry's industrial infrastructure had been hard hit by emphasizing the need for an expedient resumption of factory production for the war effort. Alderman Halliwell announced that the National Emergency Committee's daily sessions had been resumed.

On the same day, a 19-year-old fire-watcher appeared at Coventry Police Court to face charges, which, under different circumstances, would have assumed the comedy and tragedy of theatre. Over three days during Christmas, the young man admitted, he had broken into the offices of E. C. S. (Coventry) Ltd on Much Park Street, where he pilfered whisky, brandy, gin, wine and champagne to the value of £14 18s 3d – a staggering amount in today's terms, and small wonder that it had taken him three days to execute. On New Year's Day, police discovered a pile of empty bottles at the bottom of the accused's garden in Cheylesmore. With such evidence stacked against him, and after first denying any knowledge of the alleged theft, the man admitted stealing the alcohol, adding that he 'drank the lot'.

10–11 APRIL 1941

On Maundy Thursday, 10 April, the German bombers returned. At 9.40 p.m. that night, the not uncommon sound of air-raid sirens pierced the still night. It quickly became evident, however, that Birmingham was the Luftwaffe's main target. For seven unrelenting hours, the German bombers pummelled three districts in the Birmingham area. They then switched their attentions to Coventry, in an extremely intense raid that lasted three hours. In one of the worst raids in the West Midlands, the already shell-shocked Coventry shared with Birmingham the brunt of the Nazi onslaught.

The experiences gleaned from almost a year of aerial attacks were now paying dividends, and in spite of widespread damage to property, as dawn broke the fire services had the large fires under control. Another 170 fatalities were added to those of Tuesday's raid.

The third of Coventry's famous trio of spires was all that was left of Christ Church. Incendiary bombs, as with St Michael's six months ago, reduced the church building to a burned-out shell that was subsequently demolished. Today, the site is being developed in the shadow of the nineteenth-century spire, at 230 feet, the shortest of the city's trio. St Michael's spire is the tallest at 295 feet, while that of Holy Trinity rises 237 feet.

Searching bomb debris for life. (Photos Ministry of Information and Gerry van Tonder)

At Holy Trinity, a high-explosive bomb went off against the east boundary wall, shattering the church's east window and damaging the altar. Another bomb also missed the church, exploding next to the library. The post office on Hertford Street was gutted, losing the top floor.

On Trinity Street, a stick of high-explosive bombs narrowly missed the Hippodrome, most landing in Lady Herbert's Garden, but also sparing Swanswell Gate.

Old Hippodrome and the crenelated Swanswell Gate. (Photos Rob Orland and Gerry van Tonder)

Lady Herbert's Garden and Swanswell Gate. (Photos Rob Orland and Gerry van Tonder)

In Warwick Row, a street shelter took a direct hit, killing twenty-eight occupants. With the Daimler and Alvis works major Luftwaffe targets in Radford, it was inevitable that Radford School would be hit. During the raid, the school burned to the ground. Again, there was widespread damage to domestic properties. As always feared, the lot of the providers of emergency and wartime services was fraught with danger. Four wardens' posts were completely destroyed, killing three. A further nine wardens were injured in the Radford Zone. On the Tuesday, two AFS firemen were killed, while on Thursday, five AFS firemen perished when their post at Tutton's Garage on Little Park Street in the Lower Stoke and Cheylesmore Zone took a direct hit. Over the two days, thirty-seven AFS volunteers were injured.

Reminiscent of the November raids, showers of incendiary devices and parachuted marker flares preceded the dropping of heavy-calibre, high-explosive ordnance. Despite having to run the gauntlet of sustained heavy anti-aircraft fire from the ground, the sorties included the employment of dive-bombing tactics. It was slight consolation for the long-suffering Coventry, but official sources at the time issued a communiqué stating that RAF fighters had brought down nine German bombers in the West Midlands, while anti-aircraft guns had accounted for another.

The city centre was devoid of traffic, with those routes not made impassable by debris or cratered cordoned off by the civil authorities. Not for the first time, a number of shopping streets suffered badly in the latest raid. Temporary structures erected by retailers in an attempt to continue with their livelihood, found their businesses levelled. There were also instances where shops repaired after the raids of the Tuesday night were again hit.

Large numbers of troops, armed with rifles and digging tools, again flooded the city. One of their jobs was to guard the city centre perimeters from casual visitors – only essential services and those with confirmed business in the city centre were allowed to pass.

Owen Owen store a burned-out shell. (Photo Rob Orland)

(Photo courtesy © Rolls Royce Heritage Trust, Derby)

In the two raids, more than thirty factories sustained bomb damage. The sprawling Armstrong Siddeley works to the south of the city centre, had the gas turbine machine shop and car products store partly destroyed (above). Damage at Daimler's Radford site was extensive. Large sections of the works were destroyed, including the gun turret shop and scout car manufacturing unit. The Alvis works, manufacturers of aero-engine parts for Rolls-Royce's Merlin engines, had its tool-room section put out of production. Rover's test house in Red Lane was rendered unusable, while Morris Motors suffered major infrastructural damage.

Several of the city's public shelters took direct hits, raising fears of large numbers of casualties. At one site, the work of a rescue party was severely hampered by burning debris cascading down on them from adjoining buildings.

Food rationing for victims of the raid was lifted, while, once more, townspeople were reminded to boil water and milk before consumption. Trading licence restrictions were also temporarily wavered, to allow, for example, butchers to also stock and trade is groceries and bread.

As buses and trucks from hundreds of miles away were seen to be operating in the city to complement hamstrung city services, Coventry's mayor, Alderman J. A. Moseley clearly understood the need for solidarity in his wrecked city, his people now visibly showing evidence

Lady Godiva – a memorial to resistance. (Photos Rob Orland and Tanya Dedyukhina)

of despair and desperation. *The Midland Daily Telegraph* of that Easter Saturday carried Moseley's message of encouragement:

> When the attack of the 14th November occurred I had only been Mayor for five days, but I knew enough of the people of Coventry to be assured that, whatever ordeal came to them, they were capable of facing it.
>
> At that time I said two things which I repeat now. First, that I never felt prouder of the people of Coventry, and second, that whatever Hitler tries to do, he cannot break their spirit. An American journalist who came to Coventry in November, after going about the city and seeing things for himself, said to me, 'Hitler can't beat you people,' and in those words he uttered what I know is the truth.
>
> THE RAIDERS HAVE FAILED
> The new attack has hit us hard. It would be folly to disguise that, but equally folly to exaggerate it. I am deeply grieved at the suffering and the loss which has come to so many, and I am profoundly disgusted at the brutal and indiscriminate nature of the attack. Clearly, the raiders aimed at destroying the public morale, and there they most definitely have failed. There is certainly a change in the feeling of the people, but it is a change to a quiet anger and a deepened determination.
>
> The shining courage of the people will, in my belief, be a treasured memory to Coventry for generations to come.

Memorial to Coventry's citizens who lost their lives in the Blitz. (Photo Gerry van Tonder)

15 APRIL 1941

On Tuesday, 15 April, mourners congregated at the London Road Cemetery to inter in mass graves 394 victims of what had become known as the Holy Week bombings. To coincide with this, it was announced that a special section would be set aside as a war cemetery in which only the 'victims of Nazi terrorism will be buried'. Alderman Moseley, in announcing council's

Prime Minister Churchill in the ruins of the Cathedral. (Photos David McGrory and Gerry van Tonder)

decision, indicated that it was the desire of the civil administration to erect a memorial on the site, which would be laid out and maintained along the lines of the First World War cemeteries in France and Belgium. Thousands of mourners filed past the trenches, freshly dug in the red clay, in which plain elm caskets had been neatly stacked, each displaying a paper identification label.

An emotional Bishop of Coventry, Dr Mervyn Haigh, said quietly, 'This country, happily, as your presence here to-day shows, is not yet under the heel of Hitler, and, please God, it is never going to be.' (*The Midland Daily Telegraph*, 16 April 1941)

The following day, during an extensive visit to the city, the Duchess of Gloucester paid her respects at the fresh mass graves, where she laid a basket of lilies and daffodils.

SEPTEMBER 1941–SEPTEMBER 1942

On 26 September 1941, Prime Minister Winston Churchill toured Coventry in an open car, lauding its citizens for their courage and forbearance. In February the following year, the King and Queen paid their second visit, during which they were shown the first plans to rebuild the city.

Occasionally, there were still a few random small-scale raids, but the number of air-raid alerts started to taper off. On 30 July 1942, Coventry suffered its final bombing fatalities of the war when three people were killed on Bull's Head Lane.

The last bombs fell on 31 August that year, landing in the Avon Street and Alfall Road area.

The third anniversary of the outbreak of the Second World War was a seminal occasion in the history of the city of Coventry. The horrific and costly German bombing of this West Midlands city appeared to be over. Declared a National Day of Prayer, many made the spiritual pilgrimage to St Michael's Cathedral. Inside, they had to clamber on top of rubble that still lay awaiting removal within the charred and cracked walls. In the shadow of the symbol of triumph that the cathedral's spire had come to represent, Dr Mervyn Haigh, gave his last address as Bishop of Coventry, stressing the need for 'a united people who trust each other all the way.'

In the years that lay ahead, these valedictory words became the single strongest mantra of the new cathedral.

6
RISE OF THE PHOENIX

'In one night the entire site is cleared for this regeneration, and it rests with the fortunes of war and the desires of a great people to see it accomplished.'
  Coventry City Architect Donald Gibson, Royal Society of Arts, London, 3 December 1940

In 1940, the 32-year-old Gibson, Coventry's first architect and planning officer, compared the city's catastrophic destruction by Luftwaffe bombs to a forest fire, which, evil at the time, brought greater riches and architectural beauty. Revealing that 'over a year and a half ago' he had prepared a revolutionary plan for a new open-plan city centre.

At great expense to the city, Nazi Germany's war machine had become the unlikely facilitator of his dream:

> Many citizens had despaired of having a dignified and fitting city centre. High land values, the delays involved by town planning legislation, together with a lack of plan for the central area, made it seem impossible.

(Photo Gerry van Tonder)

Model of the New Coventry, showing the Central Market and Commercial Buildings. Scale 24' to the inch.

ASSETT-LOWKE LTD
MODEL MAKERS
NORTHAMPTON

(Courtesy Rob Orland)

Now, in a night, all this is changed.

Instead of a tightly packed mass of buildings of every description, there are just burned out ruins. Desolation, debris, and ashes are everywhere.

I prepared a civic centre scheme which, grouped round the two noble mediaeval churches, embodied all the public buildings in one ordered conception, at the same time suggesting a central park space, which is so badly needed.

The Midland Daily Telegraph, Wednesday, 4 December 1940

Gibson suggested that, with an ultimate cessation in hostilities, the city's industrial power base so efficient in war production, turn to housing construction using the same 'beautiful materials' in aircraft manufacture: steel, duralumin and light alloys. He propounded the use of precast concrete to which cladding or ashlar could be affixed.

Integral to his radical vision, and 'just as in a modern car', houses should be designed to 'live the same useful life'. For Gibson, this meant a maximum of thirty years.

Ultimately, the city centre provided planner and architect alike with a slate wiped clean by Hitler's bombs. On the corner of Greyfriars Lane and Broadgate, the Doric columns of the erstwhile National Provincial Bank, now NatWest, provide one of few landmarks from the past (see following page). The King's Head Hotel on the next corner has gone, and Hertford Street no longer runs into Broadgate – brick buildings have closed the intersection. Owen Owen is now gone.

(Photos Rob Orland and Gerry van Tonder)

(Photos Rob Orland and Gerry van Tonder)

(Photos Rob Orland and Gerry van Tonder)

At the intersection of Hales and Bishop streets (above), a policeman stands astride tramlines directing traffic. The fourteenth century stone church, place of worship to the ancient St John's Hospital, later to become the Old Grammar School, has also survived everything that history could throw at it. Along Bishop Street, however, the old buildings have been replaced, and in the background, concrete lift towers mark the latest high-rise development in the city.

Within weeks of the Holy Week raids, the issue of rebuilding became contentious and divisive. Financing the reconstruction soon overshadowed the plans for a 'beautiful and healthy' city. The controversial People's Common Law Parliament warned that, under the prevailing financial system, if the people of Coventry 'enriched themselves by building a beautiful city, financial perversion would turn their real wealth of homes, streets, and noble buildings into debt to be paid by them and future generations'. It added that 'rates and taxes would condemn the people to poverty'. Led by the Reverend Paul Stacy, a group of Coventry's clergy appealed to the local MP to make representation in parliament for a credit scheme to renovate the city 'without leaving a trail of debt behind'.

Pedestrianized precincts, hemmed in by rising brick and concrete structures, would become the new trend, with Smithford Way, Market Way and Hertford Street today bearing very little resemblance to those of the pre-war era.

Certain members of council advocated a process whereby individual property owners would submit claims to the War Damage Commission. As an adjunct to this, the town clerk believed that council give consideration, under the findings of the Uthwaite Committee, for it to acquire properties within designated bombed areas based on a 31 March 1939 valuation.

Smithford Street. (Photos Rob Orland and Gerry van Tonder)

In the interim, independent fundraising had already commenced for the rebuilding of the cathedral and the hospital. In a reference to architect Donald Gibson's plans accepted in principle at the previous meeting, Alderman O. M. Flinn, possibly more out of frustration at the indecisiveness of his colleagues, declared that unless the overall rebuilding scheme was amended, then 'the centre of the city would remain as it is today'.

In October 1943, in presenting his annual budget, chairman of the city's finance committee, Alderman Hodgkinson, suggested that £20 million would be 'a reasonable figure to give a reasonable slice of redevelopment.' Many councillors held firm that their city had suffered 'enemy action which was not of their choosing', so should not be expected to shoulder the full burden of reconstruction.

In February the following year, the Bishop of Coventry, Dr Neville Gorton, announced that plans for the rebuilding of St Michael's Cathedral were underway. Well-known and respected British architect Sir Giles Scott had created a design for a place of worship in which the altar was in the centre of the church. Embodied in the spiritual fabric of the new structure was the unity of Anglican and so-called free churches – a people's cathedral. Both the bishop and the provost, who was in the cathedral as it burned out of control, agreed, however, that the city's priority was for the building of houses and hospitals.

By the end of 1945, the global conflagration had ended, but in rubble-strewn Coventry the rhetoric about the city's structural future continued unabated. The only possible exception was in October when Gibson came up with revised plans which went on display at the 'Coventry of the Future' exhibition.

(Photos New York Times Paris Bureau Collection and Gerry van Tonder)

A transformed post-war Broadgate. (Photo Rob Orland)

With the immediate post-war return to Westminster of Labour, the new Minister of Town and Country Planning, Lewis Silkin, was invited to officiate at the opening of the exhibition. The Coventry Chamber of Commerce endorsed the latest plans, and with Labour returned to lead council with an increased majority, it appeared that, at last, actual rebuilding would commence.

On Victory Celebrations Day on 8 June 1946, Gibson's Levelling Stone was in place on the Precinct, carrying a carved phoenix by Trevor Tennant, a symbol of the resurrection of the city. The formal layout of Broadgate was completed in 1947, followed two years later by the positioning of the bronze Lady Godiva. In May 1948, the future queen, Princess Elizabeth officially opened Broadgate Square, and laid the foundation stone for Coventry's first new building, Broadgate House. A year later, the final plans for a ring road were approved.

The new centre was characterized by a structural grid that allowed Gibson a degree of flexibility to his architecture in what was essentially modernist, no frills brick structures, which, however, clashed when they met classical designs such as the National Provincial Bank. The influence of post-1932 Swedish architecture is evident in the brick façades, with varying four-sided window boxes often providing the only aesthetic enhancement. As property owner and town planner, the city council was able to ensure that other architects adhered to the Gibson template, particularly in terms of form and building materials employed.

In the decade following the war, Coventry's burgeoning motor and engineering works, having largely reverted to non-war production, fuelled a healthy growth in the city's economy. By the early 1960s, those very factories that Hitler almost destroyed were employing a massive 70 per cent of Coventry's population, which had now grown to just over 300,000. The wealth was tangible. In the twelve years up to 1960, private car ownership grew by a staggering 320 per cent.

Reconstruction, the circular edge of the Coventry Retail Market on the left. (Photo Rob Orland)

Council now came increasingly under pressure to keep pace with this expansion in the provision of community infrastructure such as transport, health and education. By 1955, Gibson's master plan had become largely redundant.

In 1955, Arthur Ling succeeded Gibson. The transition was quickly evident as concrete, both in structure and cladding, started being used. Coventry's first high-rise appeared and the inner ring road was significantly redesigned. Ling did, however, perpetuate Gibson's designs of car-free pedestrianized shopping precincts in the heart of the city. An upgraded ring road and multi-storey carparks would ensure that this remained so.

By 1960, the implementation of the master plan, based on precincts, was well underway, including construction of Shelton Square on Market Way.

Ling also started to add decorative colour to the hitherto relatively sober façades of Coventry's new buildings, such as the Locarno dancehall, which later became the City Library. Vibrant mosaic and tiled murals appeared alongside large, glazed structures. Tower blocks of flats – Mercian House and Hillman House – completed precinct boundaries, providing inner-city accommodation for 'professional people without families'. In a dramatically and rapidly changing skyline the three-spire status as the city's sole sentinels was being usurped.

Tucked away behind the Arcade and Lower Precinct, the new circular City Market was characterized by stark, uncompromising, V-shaped concrete columns and roofing beams. The sheer brutalism of the interior was tempered with farming and industrial murals painted by

Coventry University's Alan Berry Building facing the cathedral across University Square. (Photo Showmanradio)

art students from Dresden, the city in Germany that had suffered the same aerial destruction as Coventry during the war.

In 1964, Terence Gregory took over at the helm of city architecture. An early attempt by the new incumbent at cheap, high-density housing in the city in the form of four-storey blocks of flats constructed from precast concrete panels atop concrete columns, sullied the trend of earlier designs. Gregory's uninspiring use of concrete was repeated with the multi-storey flats of Vincent Wyles House. They would be the last of Coventry's experiment with private high-rise accommodation.

Arguably, the institutions of tertiary education had – and continue to have – the greatest impact on the city's modern architectural profile. Gregory had a vision of an inner-city university, something that not always met with favour from the traditionalists within council.

Coventry University has its roots in 1843 when the Coventry School of Design was established in the city. In 1954, it was retitled the Coventry College of Art, and as the institution's curricula kept pace with a city in seemingly perpetual transition since the dark days of the Second World War, in 1970 it became the Lanchester Polytechnic and, in 1980, the Coventry Polytechnic. In 1992, the polytechnic was granted the authority to award degrees and retitled Coventry University.

University House, administrative hub of the University of Warwick to the south-west of the Coventry city centre. (Photo Showmanradio)

With local and international status as a 'modern' university, the campus is situated among some of the city's oldest buildings, including the iconic St Michael's. Colourful student residences dominate Coventry's skyline more and more with each passing year.

The city's other 'modern' university is the University of Warwick, with its 710-acre campus on the city's outskirts. Established in 1965, the eclectic architectural styles of the campus range from the 1960s' contemporary style, to the ultra-modern lines of the Warwick Arts Centre, the largest of its kind in the Midlands.

By the late 1960s and early 1970s, the appearance of the city centre continued to evolve. Hertford Street was pedestrianized and the shops to the north-west levelled to make way for canopied and stepped two-storey shop units. To the north of the Barracks Car Park, the twin, multi-storey towers of the Coventry Point office block sprang up, Gregory adhering to his fondness of concrete evident in the white-flint, concrete-aggregate external finish.

Ford's Hospital interior, shown here with an image of a wartime warden and the ubiquitous stirrup pump, has been faithfully rebuilt. (Photos Ministry of Information and Gerry van Tonder)

The sentiments of Coventry's citizenry remained largely tacit, with just occasional stalwarts of the traditional voicing their concerns in the *Telegraph*. Crucially, much of Coventry's original architecture, having survived Hitler's onslaught, was being lost to either demolition or by being veiled in modern new materials. With the image that the retail industry presented to the consumer becoming highly critical to marketing themselves, very few of the old buildings were deemed attractive enough to meet their prerequisites. Even then, the neighbouring Albert and Victoria buildings on Queen Victoria Road, initially adapted for retail and leisure purposes, fell foul to the whims of 'modern' architecture. The latter was demolished, while what remained was either cloaked in the brown/orange hues of Hornton stone or the entrances modernized with glass and curtain walls. For many, the ultimate insult was the covering up by brick of the grand baroque façade.

Perhaps the greatest tragedy was the scant regard shown by architect and council alike for the future of old and ancient Coventry. While successive Town and Country Planning acts of the immediate post-war 1940s required the responsible local authorities to draw up detailed lists of buildings and structures 'of special architectural or historic interest' for prescribed protection, Coventry's first lists only appeared in 1955. In the interim, only the historical icons of the city, such as its medieval churches and hospitals and city wall ruins, were given preferred status.

Many listed buildings, having survived the Blitz, had to make way for the new pedestrianized precincts and buildings. St Mary's Guildhall, and Ford's and Bond's hospitals were among the few that were spared and faithfully restored. Ford's Hospital on Greyfriars Lane, was completely restored to its ancient quaintness.

(Photos Rob Orland and Gerry van Tonder)

On this site stood St. Michaels Baptist Church from 1856 until November 1940 rebuilt at Quinton Park, Cheylesmore, Coventry. New building completed on original foundations 1991.

(Photos Rob Orland and Gerry van Tonder)

On the corner of Hay and Pepper lanes stands the Golden Cross (previous page), one of Coventry's oldest public houses. Originally built in the late sixteenth century, the timber-framed Tudor structure has, over time, undergone considerable modification. On the opposite corner, on Bayley Lane, once stood St Michael's Baptist Church (pictured above). Destroyed in the Blitz, a modern stone building became the Golden Cross's new neighbour. Timber from the church's bell tower was used in one of the Golden Cross's restoration projects.

Medieval buildings from Much Park Street were translocated to Spon Street, albeit with disregard for historical integrity. Startlingly, a survey of Coventry's timber-framed buildings conducted in 1965, revealed that only 34 of the original 100 listed in 1958 and the 240 that had survived the Blitz, remained.

In the housing estates, some 8,500 – 7 per cent – of Coventry's residential properties were totally destroyed during the Blitz. The post-war exponential growth in Coventry's economy was reflected in a sharp increase in the demand for housing. Gibson had already left his signature design in Canley in the form of flat-roofed, red-brick houses, each sporting precast concrete porches.

Central government's failed attempt at providing a national housing solution saw a modest number of British Iron and Steel Federation (BISF) Type A prefabricated houses being erected in Coventry. Gibson, on the other hand, was determined that Coventry would not also fall victim to mile upon mile of architecturally repetitive rows of semidetached houses. Greens would feature as suburban centrepieces, facilitating greater architectural innovation, such as in the new Tile Hill Estate, where, on Jardine Crescent, a three-storey block of flats curves in

Typical steel prefabricated
post-war houses.
(Photo Simon Trew)

harmony with a central, circular green. Community centres and services would also follow the modernist brick and concrete styles of the inner city.

While only five schools were destroyed in the Blitz and several others damaged, the expansion of the city's population and a post-war rise in the birth rate saw the demand for secondary school places double from 1946 to 1951. Here too, Gibson determined that primary schools would be at the nexus of neighbourhoods and within walking distance. Taking into consideration the need for expediency, Gibson again turned to prefabricated building methods, comprising a lightweight steel framework to which would be affixed precast concrete panels. Importing concepts from Hertfordshire, the school buildings featured glazed façades and colourful panels.

Coventry was not the only British city to suffer major bomb damage during the Blitz of 1940–41. At the end of the war, however, the route of reconstruction that Coventry pursued diverged from that of the other bombed cities. Not only was Coventry the first provincial city to be bombed, but hers was the only cathedral destroyed by German bombs. This status immediately drew the Royal family's empathy, the monarch visiting the city only two days after the 14 November raid. Early in 1942, the King and Queen Elizabeth returned, at which time he endorsed Gibson's vision for the future city. They would visit again in April 1951. Coventry had acquired a uniquely special status.

An expression of rebirth, reconciliation, remembrance, and the strength and courage of the human spirit in overwhelming adversity would have to be manifested in a new cathedral, an international icon that embodied the resurrection and the victory over evil. As early as 1944, Giles Scott's plan for a traditional Gothic design was shunned by the majority of Coventry's clergy. The future of the cathedral ruins was also debated. Gibson and his young protégés clamoured for modernity.

The only solution proved to be an open competition, held in 1951, when Basil Spence's design was adjudged the winner. Spence astutely avoided controversial schools of thought, electing to go for a 'stripped Gothic' design, the building touching the old cathedral at right angles. Plain, unadorned concrete columns, walls and roof vault provided a modernist and minimalistic interior, the walls broken at regular intervals with multi-coloured stained-glass windows, the content geometric and abstract (pictured opposite).

Above: (Photo Gerry van Tonder)

Right: (Photo Gerry van Tonder)

(Photo Gerry van Tonder)

The cathedral would remain roofless and unchanged, a memorial to the past. The historic spire would dominate the whole complex, while Jacob Epstein's triumphant St Michael – standing over the vanquished, supine devil – towers over the steps leading to both old and new cathedrals (pictured above).

The spire of St Michael's, seen here from a dated Pepper Lane (pictured opposite), is arguably the most tangible monument to the resilience of the people of Coventry.

In the 1970s and 1980s, Coventry's industrial might was waning as the motor car and engineering giants started to close down. In the latter decade, the city's local authorities relinquished its control over property development. Independent private investors were encouraged and welcomed, catapulting the city into a new era of architectural freedom divorced from the constraints of open-space development of the Gibson and Ling eras.

Gibson's shops on Broadgate and Smithford Way were replaced by the modern Cathedral Lanes and West Orchards shopping centres. Road widths were reduced by up to a third to make way for new properties as available space within the ring road became a relative scarce commodity.

The momentum of Coventry's architectural revolution sped into the new millennium, relegating Gibson and Ling to the annals of history. In came the 'tin industrial shed' style of architecture, and high-rise university student residences, pushing hard against the ring road.

Had Hitler's Luftwaffe not so demonstrably 'redesigned' the heart of the city of Coventry, then the relatively small city centre would have remained quintessentially English, the preserve of the whole architectural spectrum from medieval to late Victorian, listed, protected and cherished.

(Photos Rob Orland and
Gerry van Tonder)

(Photo Gerry van Tonder)

ACKNOWLEDGEMENTS

Without the magnanimous assistance from dedicated Coventry historians, David McGrory and Rob Orland, I do wonder if this book would have made it this far. It would certainly have taken considerably longer without them. On a bitterly cold Saturday, Dave and Rob gave me an incredibly informative historical tour of their city, the emphasis on the Blitz. In the following weeks and months, both gentlemen generously gave me whatever photographs I wished to use from their collections – at no cost. In an era where everything seems to come at a price, for me the biggest reward has been to share knowledge and material through a passion for our mutual interest in preserving history wherever we can. Dave and Rob, thank you so very much.

My sincere thanks, as always, to Colonel Dudley Wall, very dear friend, historian, collector of militaria par excellence, and artist, for continuing to produce such magnificent drawings of military equipment for my books.

Not for the first time, Peter Collins and Peter Barnes of the Rolls-Royce Trust in Derby have provided invaluable original material, including photos and a bomb-strike map of the Armstrong Siddeley Works in Coventry. I am truly grateful.

To my good friend Alan Doyle who unstintingly sources or retrieves material for me at the National Archives at Kew, London.

I wish to acknowledge, with profound gratitude, the Coventry Transport Museum as a significant treasure house of the bicycle, motorcycle and vehicle industries that not only generated considerable wealth for the local economy, but, tragically, also attracted the destructive attentions of Nazi Germany. The professionalism employed to create such an expansive and comprehensive array of displays is as good as it gets.

To Neil Holmes, fellow author of the Blitz, thank you for your time freely given to work on my Photoshop skills, or rather, lack of.

Finally, to Claire Hopkins, thank you for your belief in me, without which this would not have happened.

BIBLIOGRAPHY

British Newspaper Archive, www.britishnewspaperarchive.co.uk

Churchill, Winston, *The Second World War*, Vol. II, 'Their Finest Hour' (The Reprint Society, London)

Clitheroe, G. W., *Coventry Under Fire* (British Publishing Company, Gloucester, first published 1987)

Farrington, Karen, *The Blitzed City: The Destruction of Coventry, 1940* (Aurum Press, London, 2015)

McGrory, David, *Coventry's Blitz* (Amberley, Stroud, 2015)

ABOUT THE AUTHOR

Born in Southern Rhodesia, now Zimbabwe, full-time historian and published author, Gerry van Tonder, came to Britain in 1999.

Specializing in military history, Gerry has authored *Rhodesian Combined Forces Roll of Honour 1966–1981*, *Book of Remembrance: Rhodesia Native Regiment and Rhodesian African Rifles*, *North of the Red Line* (South African Defence Forces border war), and the co-authored, definitive *Rhodesia Regiment 1899–1981*. Gerry presented a copy of the latter to the regiment's former colonel-in-chief, Her Majesty the Queen.

For Pen and Sword's recently introduced new 'Military Legacy' series, Gerry has written *Nottingham's Military Legacy*, the first title in the series, and *Sheffield's Military Legacy*.

He has also had published the first title in Pen and Sword's new 'Cold War' series, *The Berlin Blockade: Soviet Chokehold on Berlin and the Great Allied Airlift 1948–49*. This has been followed with *Malayan Emergency: Triumph of the Running Dogs 1948–1960*, *Red China: Moa crushes Chiang's Kuomintang, 1949*, *North Korea Invades the South: Across the 38th Parallel*, the first volume of six dealing with battles of the Korean War, and *SS Einsatzgruppen: Nazi Death Squads 1939-45*.

Gerry has also written on British local history, including *Derby in 50 Buildings*, *Chesterfield's Military Heritage* and *Mansfield Through Time*.

INDEX

Numbers in italics indicate both text and photograph on the page. Parenthesis (curved brackets) are used for clarity. Street names are organised in this index by borough.